THE
SHOW IT
LOVE
WORKOUT

Celebrate the Body You Have,
Get the Body You Want

KACY DUKE
with Selene Yeager

Mc
Graw
Hill

New York Chicago San Francisco Lisbon London Madrid Mexico City
Milan New Delhi San Juan Seoul Singapore Sydney Toronto

Library of Congress Cataloging-in-Publication Data

Duke, Kacy.
    The show it love workout : celebrate the body you have, get the body you want / Kacy Duke with
Selene Yeager.
        p.   cm.
    Includes index.
    ISBN 978-0-07-149446-5 (alk. paper)
    1. Exercise.   2. Physical fitness.   3. Health.   I. Yeager, Selene.   II. Title.

RA781.D928   2008
613.7′1—dc22   2007020141

1 2 3 4 5 6 7 8 9 10 11 12 13 14 15 16 17 18 19 20 21 22 23 24 25 26 27   WCT/WCT   0 9 8 7

ISBN 978-0-07-149446-5
MHID   0-07-149446-4

Interior photographs © by Beth Bischoff
Outfits designed by Herve Legere (cover) and Norma Kamali (interior)
Fashion styling by Kithe Brewster
Hairstyling by Dorian Dade (cover) and Amoy Pitters (interior)
Makeup by Makeup by Mario
Interior design by Think Design Group

McGraw-Hill books are available at special quantity discounts to use as premiums and sales promotions, or for use in corporate training programs. For more information, please write to the Director of Special Sales, Professional Publishing, McGraw-Hill, Two Penn Plaza, New York, NY 10121-2298. Or contact your local bookstore.

This book is printed on acid-free paper.

∽

For my mother. *You let me fly when I didn't have my wings; you protected me when I thought I was grown and alone. You love and support me like a beautiful calm day. I love you, Mommy.*

For my father. *Thank you for teaching me the power and grace of unconditional love.*

For my son, Milan. *My birthday baby! We have been through thick and thin together. Thank you for your love and affection. Because of you, I made it!*

For my beloved sister Linda. *How lucky I am to have been able to tap into the wisdom and strength of such a powerful and inspiring big sister. With boundless gratitude, appreciation, and love.*

For my big sister Peaches (Connie). *The first goddess I ever met! From buying me my first bike to teaching me to wear eyeliner, your grace and poise inspire me to this day.*

For my brother, Kithe. *The best fashion stylist in the world! Thank you for holding me together during the hard years and dressing me so beautifully. To this day you're still by my side, making sure I never lose my glamour.*

For Enrico Pizzicarola. *Although we were very young, you were a supportive husband and a great father. Thank you for building my first workout studio and putting me on the path to a health and fitness career. I owe it all to you.*

For my sweetheart, Allel. *I found in you the most loving and supportive soul mate and a true friend.*

For Greg Russell, my good friend and mentor. *Thank you!*

For Denzel Washington. *Thank you for helping build my career with support, loyalty, and friendship.*

For Giuseppe Cipriani. *Thank you for saving my life.*

∽

Contents

Acknowledgments

Special thanks to the following people, in the order they appeared in my life:

Anne Windsor, for so many years you have been my beacon of light in a sea of changes and my personal Christopher Columbus shouting, "Look, Kacy, land!" just when I thought I was about to drown.

Esther Flores, my godmother, my friend, my introduction to the Goddess. You have been my anchor.

Tony LeRoy, because of you and your guidance, I'm living my life with ease, joy, blessings, and glory! Thank you for helping me to find the greatness in being me.

Dani Pedlow, your intuitive perspective and prayers for me have kept me lifted and loved. Thank you, my friend.

Kirk Allen Johns, thank you for believing in my vision and helping me define my philosophy:

I Am so grateful to you and so happy we met.

I Can see us being friends for life.

I Do love you!

Elizabeth Papachristou, thank you for being a great assistant, always cool under pressure, and never starstruck.

Esmond Harmsworth, literary agent and all-around good guy, thank you for seeking me out and encouraging me to write this book, holding my hand every step of the way.

Selene Yeager, I am so blessed to have found such a creative and talented woman to be my cowriter. The way you channeled me was truly a spiritual experience. This book could not have been done without you.

Yvenne King, you gave birth to Kacy Duke, the businesswoman. You truly are the best attorney one could wish for.

Sante D'Orazio, you are the Great Zeus of photography, always making women look so beautiful. Thank you for giving me my Venus moment . . . I love you B.D.!

Beth Bischoff, your photography elevates the art form of the human body. Thank you for letting me into your world.

Jessica Fishman, M.S., RD, CDN, for providing the nutrititonal analyses for the recipes.

Many thanks also to the countless clients and students who graciously trusted me with their bodies. Without their trust and confidence, I would not be who I am today.

And to Deborah Brody and McGraw-Hill; Amoy Pitters; Makeup by Mario; Dr. David Colbert; Julianne Moore; Roberta Flack; Suzanne de Passe; Pamela Hanson; Kim Sevy; Pippa Cohen; Dean Harris; Nancy Arann; Justice Vasquez; Bethann Harderson; my crew (Ellen, Grace, Ariane, Anthony, Ludmilla, Inga, Tracy, Colleen); Christopher Lockhart; Naomi Campbell; Sky Nellor; Gladys Seamon; Cartina Gaines; Shirley Thomas; Dan Berger; David Rosenberg; Veronica Webb; Sphinx; Dr. Igor Gerzon; Caitlin Flaherty; Judy Taylor; Jason Frye; Jennifer Ruff; Robert Barcia; K. L. Howard-El; Equinox Fitness Club; Visual X Change; The Secret; and my Orishas, Saints, and Goddesses—with love.

—KD

I give thanks to Kacy for her light, wisdom, and laughter. You're a goddess! To Dave, my never-failing foundation. To Juniper for the endless hugs and love. To Mom and Dad for believing in me (literally) from the beginning. To Allel and Milan for nourishing our long work sessions. To Esmond and Sandra for getting the ball rolling and keeping it moving in the right direction. To Beth for bringing our story to life. To Deb and everyone at McGraw-Hill for believing in the vision and making it happen. And to God for hearing all those prayers.

—SY

Introduction

Greatness Is in You

I've trained Denzel Washington for years, helping him shape up for his demanding movie roles. Though he's blessed with beautiful genes, working out has never been his first love, so I'm accustomed to seeing his fitness levels slide between roles. At first, I thought this was simply how it was going to be training Denzel—after all, what if a role came up that demanded he gain a lot of weight? Since each role requires a different body, how could he do consistent training?

Then I realized that I'd focused on the job, not the person. Whatever Denzel needed to do for his career, he'd do. I understood that his backslides had more to do with his emotional and spiritual relationship with his body than the pressures of Hollywood, and I began a focused program of working with Denzel on his relationship with his physical self.

One day recently, while we were running the loop in Central Park, I noticed he was as fit as I'd ever seen him, even though he was coming off a hiatus. The program was beginning to work. "I'm starting to do this for me, not for the camera," he confided with that trademark wide smile. "I'm working out because I want to have a long, great life. I want to be fit and healthy for whatever comes along." Amen!

Most people start exercise programs for all the wrong reasons—because they hate their thighs or want to get rid of a spare tire. That kind of superficial, negative motivation can't sustain positive change. That's why they lose and gain the same 30 pounds over and over for years on end. (Yes, even celebrities are susceptible.) The big problem is that as soon as that ass gets a bit smaller or that spare tire recedes, people who don't love their bodies suddenly see all sorts of other things they think are wrong with their physical selves. It's been so much hard work, and they still don't have bodies they like (let alone perfect bodies!)—so out comes the cheesecake.

Women who fall into this trap get so bogged down by being unhappy with their physical selves that they block their spiritual and emotional progress. Even if they get appreciably closer to a lean body, they don't appreciate it! I believe it takes all three elements—physical, spiritual, and emotional work—to realize true success. By being honest with yourself and working hard, you can tap into your inner strength and reach your fullest potential.

Show It Love™ is a step-by-step process to appreciating and honoring your body—something all women desperately need to do *right now*. We're marrying later. We're having kids later. We're asking our bodies to be strong, sexy, powerful, and, most important, healthy well into decades when our grandmas would have just thrown on the muumuus and pulled out the rockers. Now more than ever, you need to love your body and do what's right for it. And you know what? The reward is being in the best damn shape of your life.

I Am: The Mind-Set

These days it seems like everyone wants you to be someone else. So many of the fitness mags want you to have Rebecca Romijn's thighs, Ashlee Simpson's belly, Halle Berry's booty. But they miss the most important person: you. Knowing who *you* are and what *you* need is essential to achieving lifelong fitness and embodying a physical being you truly love and feel proud of.

The plain truth is that almost any fitness program you try will work . . . at least for a little while. But after a few weeks or months, the vast majority of programs will also cease to work. The reason most programs fail to yield lasting, meaningful results: they address women on only one level—the physical. They treat us like a composite of body parts, as though we're nothing but belly, butt, and thighs, when that's only the outside—the vessel that holds our hearts and our minds. They teach us to "banish" our body instead of showing it love. In the end, it never works. Not long term. That's why women go from program to program, forever searching for the one that will "click," that will resonate with who they really are. Instead of focusing totally on the physical, the fitness program that works needs to nurture every woman's mind, feelings, and spirit.

That's why the first section of this book, I Am, is devoted to exploring your mind-set. Think of I Am as taking a complete emotional inventory. In it, you'll find all the tools you need to explore the complicated, intricate relationship you have with your body, including what you love or hate about exercise, how your mirror image makes you feel, and what drives you to the box of Triscuits instead of the gym. This level of self-awareness is especially hard for women, who are constantly looking outside themselves at other people. They compare and compete (knowingly or not) with the women around them, especially celebrities, which is the cruelest comparison of all because the only things most people know of the "rich and famous" is what they're allowed to see.

I have the privilege of working with some of the most beautiful bodies and sought-after celebrities in Hollywood—people like Bruce Willis (even sharing a magnificent Thanksgiving with him, Demi, and Ashton), Gwen Stefani, and Kirsten Dunst—and I can tell you that while they certainly have more glamorous lives than most of us, they aren't all that different otherwise. They get up and brush their teeth in the morning. They take out the trash at night. They have lives and families and hopes and fears. They worry about how they look. However, what the most successful, self-assured celebrities have that sets them aside—and what you can have too—is a strong sense of self.

That is the true foundation of a movie-star body. That is how I help my clients achieve the body of their dreams. By building a solid, emotional relationship with your body and learning to respect and honor it, you may not turn into Kristen Bell overnight, but over time you will stop being your worst critic. You'll stop all the negative self-talk and the body hate. You'll finally make measurable progress in the gym. And you'll (finally!) truly love what you see when you look in the mirror.

If you're ready for some real results, I strongly encourage you to kick back and take your time while exploring the I Am section of this book. This is your foundation. Think of it as building your dream house. You wouldn't just toss down some old sheets of plywood and plop a house on top of them. No. You'd dig deep and pour a rock-solid foundation so your beautiful construction could weather any storm and last and last, bringing you joy for the rest of your life. That's what I Am will do for your most precious shelter of all—your body.

My Personal Journey Through I Am

Even after all these years, I still revisit the principles in I Am almost every single day. As a high-profile fitness trainer in New York, I feel tremendous pressure to meet people's expectations of what I'm supposed to look like. And I'll be completely honest with you here: sometimes I don't. I am not a twig. Nor do I have bulging, cut muscles. I am solidly built, with full, feminine curves. I've also gone through many of the special rites of passage that women go through. I've been married. I've been pregnant. I'm working to be a good mother and put a kid through college. I am no longer 22. The exercises and lessons in I Am have allowed me to enjoy and respect my body throughout every stage of life and to be comfortable with who I am and what I look like in an industry that practically worships youth and perfection.

Most recently, I had a very personal setback. I had to have an ovary removed. On an emotional level, I was forced to close the door on my life as a fertile, reproductive woman. Spiritually, I wasn't motivated to go to the gym, and I wasn't sure how much I could manage physically even if I did. So I practiced what I preached. I looked myself in the mirror, and I honored my body. I thanked it for my beautiful son, Milan. I thanked my thighs and my (now slightly scarred) belly for carrying me and giving birth to so much strength and creative energy throughout the years. I showed it love. Then I told my body to get ready for the next level of adventure. I promised it that once it healed, we'd go and have fun together and do something to celebrate its strength and perseverance. I've decided I'm going to learn to swim, and I'm going to do a triathlon. That's my next step on my journey.

That is the power of I Am.

I Can: The Motivation

Once you are able to say, "I am _____" and fill in the blank with positive affirmations, you're ready to say, "I can." Part 2 of this book is all about motivation. The motivation to try something new, to show your body love, and to take it to the next level because *you* want to do it for yourself. The ultimate goal of I Can is to become your own life's motivation.

It's common knowledge that more than half of women who start an exercise program throw in the towel before six months are through. I believe that's because (1) they didn't start with a strong, emotional foundation, which I address before I even think of asking a client to step on a scale, and (2) they don't believe in themselves, so they make excuses and lose motivation. That's where I Can comes in.

Society has put so many restraints on women's thinking that they can't let their expectations fly. In I Can, you will learn firsthand the strength and potential contained in your body, no matter your shape or fitness level. My signature Woman Warrior exercise sequences will lengthen your spine so you stand tall and proud. You'll feel the power of your chest, work your legs in new ways that reveal their potential and power, and solidify your core— the creative center of your being. Spiritually emboldened, you'll see that exercise is not some mechanical set of movements you sleepwalk through for 45 minutes, two to three days a week. It's the act of screaming, "I am alive!"

Then get ready to look at food in a brand-new way. This is no diet book. I'm not going to limit your daily snacks to 15 raw almonds a day or guilt you into swearing off wine, chocolate, and Italian bread for the rest of your life. In fact, some days indulging will be exactly what you need (just wait until you taste my City Girl Trifle!). Instead, you're going to learn how to feed your body and soul. Instead of stuffing food down to quiet your feelings, you'll tune in to them and hear exactly what your body craves and needs to feel happy—and healthy.

I Can is also where you finally ditch all those tired old excuses for skipping workouts, because you simply won't need them anymore. You'll have purpose. You'll have meaningful goals. You'll be making measurable progress. And you'll look at moving and caring for your body as a way of rewarding and honoring yourself, not as a punishment for not fitting into size 0 designer jeans or blowing the diet of the day.

My Personal Journey Through I Can

My second marriage was a traumatic, abusive affair. Without digging up all those old skeletons, suffice it to say that my husband spent a whole lot more time saying, "You can't" (as in "You can't succeed in the fitness business. You can't make it on your own.") than "You can." It would have been easy to believe him, to bury my dreams under his blanket of put-downs. I could have pulled up the covers and stuffed down the potato chips. But I knew that would be the biggest disgrace I could level against the body that had brought me so far as a dancer, instructor, and trainer. Most of all, I couldn't let someone outside of myself—especially someone so negative—be the motivation for my actions.

So I left. It was initially devastating. But I healed my emotional wounds with time, oxygen, and exercise. I moved my body in powerful ways. I challenged myself. I put my goals and dreams directly in my line of sight to be my guiding light. I put the negative past where it belonged—behind me. That's where it stays, in the background as my radar. That way my experiences move forward in a positive direction while I avoid repeating past mistakes.

It's what happens when you say, "I can."

I Do: The Movement

Now that your mental and spiritual energy is going in the right direction, it's time to let your body soar! I Do, the final step of the Show It Love program, is all about working your body to its fullest potential. While most fitness books talk about whipping your body into shape, I talk about building it up and appreciating its power and strength. Make no mistake, you *can* have the tight, high butt; the flat abs; and all that physical flash. But in this program, it's not the be-all and end-all—it's the icing on the cake.

The secret is in realizing the potential of your individual physique. The moves in I Do are designed to tap into that deep physical awareness so you can realize and embrace that potential and create a beautiful, statuesque body unique to you. It's what happens when you take that powerful emotional and spiritual pedestal and build a strong, stunning sculpture on top of it. My clients accomplish physical feats and achieve lean, gorgeous body lines they never thought possible because they know and love who they are; they believe in their abilities; and they learn how to get the most out of their physical selves.

Though it comes straight from my heart, this body-love philosophy is firmly rooted in the bedrock of science. Stanford University researchers recently reported that people who start a fitness program feeling the happiest with their bodies are more than twice as likely to meet their goals as those who are the least satisfied. That's a reality I see in the people I train every single day.

Though I Do is the most physically challenging of the three sections, it is *not* about beating yourself up. So many clients come to me for the first time expecting me to kick their asses and trash their bodies. If that's what you expect, you're in for a big surprise. Sometimes realizing your fullest physical potential means doing a little less. Recently, I had a client come in who had been hitting the weights so hard day in and day out that she almost looked like a linebacker—just big, bulky muscles everywhere. She wasn't happy with how she was shaping up, but she thought that was what she was supposed to be doing—hammering her body with heavy weights—and was afraid to let up. For her, I Do was about calming down and letting her muscles relax. I told her to put down the weights and do my muscle-lengthening Woman Warrior moves instead. I look at her now and I think, "Wow." She looks amazing.

Contrary to what you've probably read a million other places, you do *not* need heavy weights to tone and strengthen your muscles. You just need to move your muscles through a range of motion that thoroughly challenges them. That's what you'll do in I Do. And your body will look, feel, and perform better than it ever has.

Finally, a finely tuned body deserves high-quality fuel. In I Do, I'll show you how best to feed your physical self for maximum energy and performance. You'll not only find all you need to know about healthy protein, carb, and fat choices, but I'll also share a few of my trade secrets.

My Personal Journey Through I Do

I have always lived a very physical life. I ran track and competed in aerobic dance competitions. I trained as a dance therapist and later worked as a Nike Body Elite personal trainer. But ironically, it wasn't until relatively recently that I really lived through my body like an athlete. Athletes aren't out there pounding themselves into the ground 100 percent of the time, 365 days a year (like I was trying to do). They stop and go and let their training wax and wane with life's rhythm and flow. It took some episodes of burnout and injury, but I eventually learned that taking your body to its highest heights means regularly laying low and allowing all that hard work to sink in. Today, I won't hesitate to take a whole week off when I need to. Sure, I may be a little soft around the edges when I return, but believe me, I get back in the game faster and stronger than if I hadn't taken the rest.

The result: I've been able to stay in top shape throughout two decades of constant challenge and change. Despite childbirth, divorce, career changes, knee surgery, 9/11, a partial hysterectomy, and everything else, both good and bad, that life has thrown my way, my body is still rocking and rolling and ready for what's next.

All it takes is saying, "I do."

Your Journey Starts Now

Now I invite you to turn the pages and start your own journey through the Show It Love system. Begin with an open heart and mind. Be honest with, but also kind to, yourself. Chances are you're coming into this book already having tried (and maybe not having been very successful with) other programs. Like many of my clients, you may be unhappy, dissatisfied, or even angry with your body. Maybe working out hasn't been much fun, let alone joyful, for you in the past. I'm going to do my best to change all that. I'll give you 100 percent. But you have to be right there with me giving 100 percent right back. That's how successful relationships work.

A lot of what you're about to read may also seem strange to you. Throughout my life, I have drawn inspiration from powerful goddesses like Isis (goddess of love and healing) and Aurora (goddess of the dawn). Despite popular notions of the word *goddess*, these women weren't just eye candy. They were brilliant. They were together. And they were seriously bad! I'll share their stories with you throughout the book, as well as morsels of ancient healing techniques in the form of meditations and herbal tinctures. Don't get nervous. I'm not trying to change anybody's religion. And I'm not all about some New Age, woo-woo hocus pocus. Experience has simply taught me that we can draw a lot of wisdom from ancient cultures, which in many cases had it more together than we do in modern times.

Even the exercises will be remarkably different from anything you've tried before. In the spirit of those strong, powerful goddesses, I created the Woman Warrior exercise sequences—flowing movements that raise your heart rate while pumping and elongating your muscles for heightened mind-body awareness and beautifully etched body lines.

Each Woman Warrior move is designed to allow you to appreciate where your body is right now and where it can go in the future. The three Woman Warrior sequences in I Am, I Can, and I Do are total body workouts that function like Pilates or the sets of strength training and endurance poses trainers teach in many gyms. The difference: they are specifically designed for women's bodies to show the grace and strength within. I encourage you to seek the gifts of each goddess—whether it's determination, victory, courage, fertility, or power—to embrace your workouts and fully develop your strength, balance, poise, and posture. With centuries of wisdom and power on your side, there's nowhere to go but up. Now let's begin your fitness quest.

I Am

YOU are more than a pair of thighs. You are more than a belly. You are a heart and a mind and a spirit. These are not separate entities that can be "fixed" the way you would tune up a car's engine or change its tires. Nor is your mind an isolated command center for your body. Your thoughts and feelings affect your body.

They affect your movement and your hunger. Likewise, how you eat and move affect how you feel and think. You are one beautiful, complete entity.

Deep down, you probably know all that. Yet as soon as you look in the mirror, I bet you start chopping yourself to pieces again. "I need to lose this gut. I need to trim these thighs." As if your belly and legs weren't part of who you are. I don't blame you. The fitness industry has been selling us all on the idea that we can fix any piece of our bodies we want without ever addressing our minds. Go to any gym across America, and you'll get the same treatment. You ask to start an exercise program and a trainer puts you on a scale, whips out a tape measure, calculates your body fat composition, puts you through some fitness tests, and then you're supposed to go get fit!

Don't buy it. Stepping on a scale will not prepare you for your fitness journey. (Ever notice how many of your friends stop going to their gyms only weeks after joining?) The way to permanent fitness is to start with a hard first step, one that does not involve getting on the treadmill or the elliptical machine: you need to take an inventory of your emotional relationship with your body.

Until you understand how you feel about your body and why, you can't make meaningful progress in improving it. The I Am phase of your journey teaches how to understand and actually love your body through a series of quizzes and exercises that cover body image and emotional eating. I believe it's a bad idea to embark on a fitness program with goals like having smaller thighs, shapelier legs, a tighter butt, or toned arms. Yes, we'll get you those things, and it's natural to want them. But if those are your only goals, you're setting yourself up for failure, because you're beginning full of negativity. When you start out with self-hatred, you're almost destined to throw up your hands and head straight for the Häagen-Dazs the moment you hit a rough spot, because you're working *against* yourself instead of *with* yourself.

This section will teach you how to set "love goals" instead of weight-loss goals. For example:

INSTEAD OF: I want my legs to look thin.
THINK: I celebrate my legs for their ability to move and carry me, and I intend to strengthen them to increase their power.

INSTEAD OF: I want to shrink my gut.
THINK: I acknowledge that my belly is the center of my creative power as a woman—the awesome power of giving birth. I celebrate my belly for this gift. I intend to nurture and work my creative center to make it stronger and to make me a stronger woman.

It'll be hard at first. You may even feel silly setting up love goals for yourself. But my 20 years of personal experience and work with successful clients have taught me that it's nearly impossible not to feel better about yourself and ultimately meet, and often even exceed, your fitness goals when you start out by showing yourself a little love.

In the I Am section, you will find:

∞ **Show It Love tools.** Throughout this section, I'll teach you how to treat your body like your best girlfriend—in an honest, playful, and empowering way. You'll find "mirror exercises," as well as affirmations and tips for maintaining body love in a culture that inspires self-hatred.

∞ **Mood food.** Those rich, smooth, dark chocolate Dove bars may feel like the answer to all life's problems (and sometimes they are just what you need), but more often than not, women overdose on feel-good foods like chips, chocolate, and ice cream to fill an emotional void that the right movement and light, wholesome foods could fill in a more healthful way. I'll show you how.

∞ **Woman Warrior series 1.** I Am includes the first Woman Warrior exercise series, which promotes body understanding and appreciation through powerful, flowing movement. I'll follow up these strengthening moves with equally inspiring (and effective) cardio routines.

Turn the page and get ready to say, "I am!"

1

Thank Your Thighs . . . and Say Good-Bye

It sounds like the most ridiculous exercise in the world. But it works like magic for making you emotionally stronger, spiritually centered, and more receptive to physical fitness. Stand in front of the mirror. Take a good look at yourself. Now thank your body and say good-bye.

I do it regularly. In fact, I did it just the other day after eating pizza and stressing about this book (yep, even trainers are human). I looked at my backside, which was taking on a life of its own, and I stood up, looked in the mirror, and said, "Thank you, thighs. Thank you, ass. Thank you for being with me while I sat in my apartment and worried instead of worked out. Thank you for getting me through part of this cold, dreary New York winter. But now it's time to get down to business. You know what we have to do. We need to get busy and get stronger for the task ahead."

Go ahead and try it. No one's looking, so there's no need to feel stupid. Stand up, look yourself square in the mirror, and say, "Thank you, butt, for

5

supporting me through those love fests with the bags of Oreos. Thank you, belly, for growing life and giving me my children. Thank you for being there for me when I wasn't always there for you. But it's time for you to step up and make a change. I need something more."

As you say the words aloud, don't be surprised if you actually start to smile at the reflection in the mirror, if you feel lighter in your heart and a growing confidence in your gut. That's the point of the exercise. By saying the words plainly, you're acknowledging (without the tone of disgust you usually reserve for your problem areas) what's making you unhappy, perhaps for the first time in a truly productive way. You're stepping up to the plate and declaring that you're ready to make a change within yourself. Your intentions become more real when you say them aloud—even if it's just to yourself.

This exercise also breaks the ice between you and your body. We tend to be oh, so serious when we're unhappy with our hips or thighs. It's like we're wearing the weight of the world, when it's actually just a few extra pounds or a little flabby muscle. It makes us ashamed. It makes us hide from ourselves. By talking to your hips and thighs one-on-one, you have a little fun with your body instead of denying it and hating it; you open yourself up to change. As you speak matter-of-factly to your body, you realize you have the strength and power to finally, really get it done.

Quiz: Your Body and You—What Have You Done for Me Lately?

Having trouble with the mirror exercises because you can't think of anything nice to say? I guarantee that no matter who you are or what kind of shape you're in, your body has seen you through some major challenges. Take this quiz and you'll see what I mean.

1 **During the past three years, I have been through _____ major life changes. (Positive changes like getting married, promotions, and relocating count too!)**

   a. 0–1

   b. 2–3

   c. 4–5

If you answered:

   a. Your life has been relatively calm. If you've been neglecting your body or abusing it with lots of late nights or eating fests with friends and family, thank it for seeing you through the good times and for being patient with you while you let it slide. Now promise it something more.

   b. Life's been a little hectic. Even if it's all been good, change is stressful. Thank your body for seeing you through the bumps in the road. If you've put on a little weight, consider it padding to cushion the ride. Now it's time to get back in fighting shape for whatever lies ahead.

   c. Man, it's been a rough time. Thank your body for seeing you through whatever you had to do to get through these past few years, whether it's been bakery binges, too much wine, not enough exercise, or all of the above. Now reassure your body that you haven't forgotten its needs while it's been taking care of yours.

2 **I am _____ years old.**

   a. under 30

   b. between 30 and 50

   c. 50+

If you answered:

   a. Pat yourself on the back. You've made it through some of the worst body-image years a woman faces during her entire life! Our 20s are also some of our most self-abusive years, filled with too little sleep, too much partying, tumultuous relationships, and maybe even eating disorders or unhealthy exercise habits. Give your body a nod of approval for seeing you through and prepare it to get healthy and strong for the demanding years that lie ahead.

b. Marriage, children, divorce, high-stress jobs, mortgages, aging parents. Damn, these are two jam-packed decades in a woman's life! If you can think of nothing else to thank your body for, thank it for carrying you through the chaos of these crazy years. This is also the danger zone for women's bodies, when they can neglect them so badly that they can set the stage for obesity, diabetes, heart disease, cancer, and other ills. Now is the time to honor your body and forge a path to physical health so you can really enjoy your golden years with full vitality.

c. You have two choices during these years. You can look behind you and feel sadness for what you've lost or never accomplished, or you can turn your eyes forward and realize that you still have the rest of your life lying at your feet. Thank your body for helping you reach this awesome milestone in life and start moving forward to prepare it for the opportunities that await you. I see women in their 50s and 60s in the club who look better than women half their age, because they continue preparing for the future instead of living in the past.

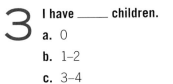

I have _____ children.

a. 0

b. 1–2

c. 3–4

If you answered:

a. Children are not the only wonderful creations women can bring forth into this world. Consider what else you've given birth to or nurtured. Have you done charity work? Spearheaded projects at work? Developed plans for your community? Consoled or nurtured a friend? Thank your body for wisdom, caring, and creative energy, and get ready to strengthen that creative core for more to come.

b. Being pregnant and nursing babies places years of special demands on your body, especially your breasts and the creative center in your belly. It's natural that those areas will show a little wear and tear when you're done. But that in no way means that you can't reclaim your strength and power and be strong and firm in those areas again. So thank your belly, breasts, and thighs for those wonderful babies, and prepare to get your body strong to raise and enjoy those kids (no matter what age they are now) in the years ahead.

c. You have some serious praising to do. Too often women with multiple children feel sad about or put down their bodies as though they were damaged goods—nothing could be further from the truth! Your breasts and belly may be drooping a little from creating and carrying the load of all those little ones, but they deserve to be honored for giving and nurturing so much life. Once you've shown them love, you can promise that you'll do something special just for them through firming and strengthening exercises.

4 If I had to choose just one thing to do for fun, it would be _____.

a. heading to dinner or a club

b. kicking back with a good book or TV show

c. going for a run or bike ride, or taking a class

If you answered:

a. Living in New York, I see plenty of women who eat out or hit some nightspot almost every night of the week. If you spend a little too much time with good food and/or good drink, you should thank your body for seeing you through your excesses. You also should acknowledge that you know it can only take so much and still be healthy and vibrant. Now make a pledge that you'll adopt some healthier lifestyle habits by choosing cleaner foods, increasing your activity, and getting the sleep and quiet time your body needs.

b. Nothing wrong with a little solitude. But spending too much time curled up on the couch can be just as unhealthy as burning the candle at both ends. Thank your body for still being with you while you engage your mind with a book or zone out in front of the TV. Then promise you'll balance those sedentary activities with plenty of movement and activity to keep it strong, flexible, and ready for action.

c. Physical activity can be a celebration of life, and exercise is definitely one of my favorite forms of entertainment. If you're very active, you definitely need to thank your body for all the running and jumping and playing it does. You also need to promise that you'll listen when it's tired and give it the rest it needs to prevent getting injured or run down.

5 **When I'm stressed out, I _____.**

a. crack open a bag of chips or cookies

b. work up a sweat

c. call a friend and vent

If you answered:

a. Join the club! I don't know a single woman who doesn't occasionally sit down with a spoon and drown her anxieties in a carton of Ben & Jerry's. As you'll see in the following chapter, what you eat elicits powerful chemical changes in your brain that literally make you feel better. But it's short-lived and not the best way to get through a bad spell. So thank your body for holding you up while you downed a bag of chips, and promise it you'll now learn and practice healthier ways to relieve stress.

b. Exercise triggers the release of feel-good, amphetamine-like drugs in your brain, so it's no wonder running feels so great when life isn't. Thank your body for staying healthy during stress-filled times, and don't forget to give it plenty of healthy food and rest in return.

c. Airing your troubles with a friend can take a load off your mind. But your body still bears the burden of the time spent sitting and stewing and stressing. Thank your body for helping keep you connected with friends and being on your side during times of need. Then promise it that you'll take action and provide it with some much-needed physical release in the future. Even better, next time you're stressed, meet your friend and go for a run or walk while you talk.

You Are What You Say You Are

Women can say the meanest things to themselves, putting themselves down as fat, lazy, clumsy—I've heard it all. But I think what bugs me the most is how women pour all these negative attributions on themselves simply because they have jiggly arms or a little fat on their thighs. Your arms and legs and belly are part of who you are, but you are not just your arms, legs, and belly. Even if your physical being is out of shape, it doesn't mean you can't be strong spiritually and emotionally. But just as you need physical exercise to maintain shapely shoulders and lean legs, you need to train your heart and mind daily to keep them positive and strong.

That's why I believe in daily positive affirmations. I hang them on my walls. I tape them to my cell phone. I keep them right in my line of sight, so I can't forget and slip back into negativity. When I'm feeling scared or my self-confidence is shaky, I stand in front of the mirror and show myself lots and lots of love. Really. I stand there and say, "Kacy, you're strong. You're capable. You're loving. You deserve to succeed and to have happiness in your life. I love you, Kacy."

That's right, I tell myself, "I love you." Not because I'm some egotist. But because I *do* love myself, flaws and all. I love myself enough to take care of myself and to want the best for myself. That's the heart of Show It Love. If you don't love yourself and don't talk nicely to yourself, how will you believe in yourself enough and care about yourself enough to reach your fullest potential? It all starts with how you talk to yourself—both out loud in front of the mirror and inside your mind all day long.

My clients often struggle with these mental exercises more than any squat or lunge, because it's more socially acceptable for women to tear themselves down than to build themselves up. We're going to change that right now. Here is a guide to creating powerful, positive affirmations.

Make a List

Grab a pen and paper (make it a nice piece of stationery or a page in a pretty journal, if possible; it's another way to show yourself some love). Now write down 15 to 20 positive adjectives to describe your attributes, talents, and strengths. Start with the phrase "I am." For example:

I am generous.	I am attractive.
I am caring.	I am patient.
I am creative.	I am persistent.
I am smart.	I am fun-loving.

Some attributes are hard to phrase as "I am." I don't want you to restrict yourself, so if you need to, use other phrasing such as "I have." The more you can come up with, the better!

I have a good sense of humor.
I have beautiful eyes.

Be sure to include adjectives that describe you emotionally, spiritually, *and* physically. Everyone has positive attributes in all three areas of self. It's critical to be positive in all three realms if you want to reach your potential.

Put It into Action

Next combine your goals with your positive attributes to come up with a list of 10 to 15 "I can" or "I will" statements. These should reflect your immediate and future goals. For instance:

I am persistent; I can lose weight.

I am strong; I can exercise every day.

I have perseverance; I can quit smoking.

I am a positive person; I can let go of guilt.

I am generous; I can allow myself pleasure.

I am resourceful, I can create a comfortable home.

I have great hair; I can feel good about how I look.

I am creative; I can cook foods that will nurture my body and my soul.

I am talented; I can get a job that will allow me the freedom to grow.

By combining your positive attributes with your goals, you're not just making empty promises to yourself. For instance, you can say, "I can quit smoking," or "I can let go of guilt," but unless you reinforce it with an "I am" statement, that little negative voice may pop up and say, "No you can't." By saying, "I am strong, so I can exercise every day," you're silencing that nagging inner critic and moving forward toward your ultimate goal.

In Your Sight, In Your Mind

When you shove something in your junk drawer, you forget all about it. (Hence the saying, "Out of sight, out of mind.") Same goes for your affirmations. If you write them down and stick them on a shelf, they'll be gone from your consciousness by the time you brush your teeth tonight. Pick the ones that are pertinent to your goals right now—be sure to include healthy eating and exercise goals, since that's the journey we're on here—and tape them in places you see every day. Here are a few of my favorite locations:

The bathroom mirror

Your armoire or dresser

Your car's dashboard

The refrigerator door

Your cell phone

The cover of your journal

On your laptop

Repeat Daily

Whenever you learn a new skill, whether it's the piano or golf, you have to practice, practice, practice. Learning to love your body is no different than any other skill. You have to rehearse it every day to make it stick.

Eventually you should be able to stand in front of a mirror, look yourself square in the eye, and say all your affirmations. Take baby steps by saying your affirmations out loud to yourself without looking in the mirror. You can do them while you wash dishes or drive in your car, but make sure you really feel them. Don't just give them lip service. You want to feel a stirring in your heart as you say the words.

Work up to saying them in the mirror. A good time is first thing in the morning, right after you've washed your face and combed your hair. Give yourself a proud smile and show yourself some love. Finally, as you get comfortable speaking to your reflection, make your affirmations part of your mirror exercises. After you thank your body for what it's done and tell it what you need to do, finish up with a few positive affirmations.

I can feel you squirming inside a little and thinking, "Kacy, just show me the damn squats and lunges. No way am I going to talk to myself in the mirror." But trust me on this. There is a reason that the vast majority of people quit exercising almost before they begin. They don't show themselves love and respect. They don't really believe. To really believe, you have to treat yourself like a best friend—or better yet, a child who depends on you for encouragement every step of the way. Growing and changing is hard. That's why we tell our kids over and over how special and capable they are. Well, right now you're in your own process of growing and changing, so you need to do the same nurturing and supporting for yourself. Top celebrities do it. Elite athletes do it. They're not that much different from you. They just believe. Keep talking to yourself. You can too.

Stand Up and Walk the Walk

When Pamela first came to me, she walked in with her shoulders slumped and back bent over like she was Atlas carrying the whole world on her shoulders. Yes, she had just turned 50, and yes, gravity had started causing a few things to droop a little here and there. But one glance at her posture told me that she was so busy looking down she couldn't even begin to see—let alone feel—her true potential.

The first thing I asked Pamela to do—and what you *must* do when you stand in front of the mirror to address yourself—was to stand up straight. As soon as she pulled her shoulders back and lifted her chin, she caught a glimpse of the strong, confident—sexy—woman she could be. Think about it. When you go to the beach, the women who catch your eye aren't necessarily the ones with the best butt or biggest boobs. They're the ones who are standing tall and strutting through the sand like they're on a runway in Paris. That kind of body confidence physically makes you look leaner. By lifting your head toward the ceiling to stand tall, you automatically pull your navel toward your spine, and you instantly look 5 to 10 pounds slimmer. More important, it has an immediate, powerful impact on your mood. You simply cannot stand tall without feeling more confident.

So I told Pamela, "Stop looking like a woman who has all her best days behind her. Reclaim that bad bitch you've buried deep inside. So much of your life is still in front of you. Don't put yourself out to pasture yet!" I'm happy to tell you that she's lost weight, sculpted her arms and booty, and even tightened and toned what we were calling the "final frontier" of her midsection. Her body is alive and awake and ready for what life (and I) am going to throw at her next. As she told me the last time I saw her, "I think there's something to this loving yourself shit." Now that's an attitude I love.

Now you try it. Stand in front of the mirror. Raise your chin so it's level with the floor and you're looking yourself straight in the eyes. Now imagine you have a light shining from your heart through your breastbone. Don't let that light shine down at the floor. You want it beaming in front of you, showing you the way to go. Roll your shoulders back gently and lift your chest. You should feel your belly tighten and your spine lengthen. Finally, picture a string gently pulling the top of your head toward the sky, so you stand and walk at your full height.

Lay Down Your Love Goals

So what is it you want to change? I know you didn't buy this book to read on the beach. If you're turning these pages, you want to put a little lift in your Levi's or tighten your arms for tank-top season. It's absolutely natural and perfectly okay to want your body to look its best. What's important for you to realize is that a gorgeous, tight body is a by-product of creating a healthy relationship with your body, not the other way around.

So many clients come in and the first words out of their mouths are, "I want thin thighs like Angelina Jolie," "I want skinnier arms," or "I need to lose 10 pounds." I don't consider those types of goals particularly constructive. Only Angelina can have her thighs. How skinny is skinny enough? And what is so magical about 10 pounds? Too often people come in with those goals and only grow increasingly dissatisfied with themselves because they don't immediately look like some movie star when they start working out.

That's why I have my clients set up love goals instead of weight-loss goals. In the spirit of the Show It Love system, love goals celebrate your body and reflect your desire for it to be stronger and more fit to carry you through life. It's like getting fit from the inside out. The primary focus is on feeling great and the end result is the tight butt, shapely shoulders, and flat abs that show how much you care for your body and how wonderful you feel on the inside.

Once you get the hang of them, love goals are easy to establish. Here are a few examples of how to reframe those tired weight-loss goals with a little love.

INSTEAD OF: I want to fit in a size 4.
THINK: I am proud of my body for all that it's accomplished. I intend to make it a strong, healthy presence, so I can further celebrate its capabilities and potential.

INSTEAD OF: I want skinny thighs.
THINK: I celebrate my legs for moving me through life. I acknowledge my thighs as the source of my strength as a woman. I will work them so I can increase their power.

INSTEAD OF: I want to lose my belly.
THINK: I recognize my belly as the center of my creative power and spirit. I celebrate it for the awesome power of giving birth. My goal is to challenge and work my creative center to make it stronger and to make me a stronger woman.

INSTEAD OF: I want thin arms.
THINK: I love my arms for granting me the ability to hold children, hug loved ones, and carry heavy loads. I intend to work my arms so they can embrace the world that much harder.

You get the idea. Now try a few of your own. Like mirror exercises and daily affirmations, love goals may take a little practice, because women aren't used to being allowed this much freedom to be positive in a society that drowns us in negative messages.

While we're addressing goals and negativity, remember that we live in a celebrity-soaked culture, so it's hard not to do some comparing and dreaming when you think about how you look and how you'd like to look. But pinning all your hopes on looking like a star is bad business for three reasons: (1) In some cases, the images of celebrities that you see are retouched or the women themselves have actually had work like plastic surgery to make them look more perfect than they really are. In other words, even *they* couldn't

Woman Warrior Inspiration

~ *Aurora* ~

Women are capable of affecting profound change. Aurora, the ancient goddess of the dawn, had the power to bring on a new day. This rosy-fingered, saffron-robed, and golden-throned goddess went up to Olympus every day to announce the coming of light to her fellow immortals. She was the sister of the sun and the moon, and the mother of the evening star. She is often shown with wings or in a chariot drawn by four horses, one of them the famous Pegasus.

Aurora transforms the world each day as the bringer of dawn. You can access her wisdom and power to do something a lot simpler: transform yourself and enjoy your body's full potential. The work will take time, but whenever your energies feel depleted, remember Aurora's long, endless journey, bringing heat and light to the world. Her power can help you replenish your energy and allow you to experience each day as a new step in your healing journey.

look that good. (2) The celebrities who do look as perfect as they appear not only have good genes (often celebrities or models for parents) but also take many hours to get that way. It's their job, and they can afford to spend three hours a day in the gym. (3) This is your body and your life, not theirs. People who spend all their energy wishing they were like some TV or movie star miss out on their own lives, and this life is the only one you have. By taking control of it and embracing the body you've been blessed with, you'll not only come closer to getting that rock-star butt and those glam-girl arms, but you'll finally have a body you truly love.

Now that's something worth shooting for.

2

Food for Your Mood

Food is essential for life. But how many of us really, consciously eat to empower our bodies to live to their fullest potential? Too often we use and abuse food as cheap entertainment or, more often, therapy. We reach for foods we think will make us happy, whether it's a pint of Häagen-Dazs or a box of Thin Mints, and we end up feeling miserable instead. Believe me, I've been there. After breaking up with my second husband, all I wanted was my bed and potato chips. That's because high-carb junk foods boost your feel-good brain chemicals . . . temporarily. But like any drug, you end up falling to earth twice as hard after the high is over.

What you eat also determines how well the Show It Love system works for you. You can do all the exercises in this book every day—heck, three times a day—but if you are spending your nights plowing through the left-overs in the fridge, all your hard work will be trashed like all those candy bar wrappers. One of my clients recently came to me frustrated because he wasn't seeing any progress. It turned out that no matter how often or how hard he worked out, he would eat so much food to "reward" himself that he would undo hours of effort in a matter of minutes. Sounds more like punishment to me, and it's certainly not the way to show your body love. This is often my biggest challenge in counseling clients—helping them feed their emotional hunger without reaching for the french fries.

The first step is acknowledging that you have an emotional relationship with food. It's nothing to be ashamed of. We all do. Once you understand the food-mood link and how you use food when you're bored, sad, frustrated, or even happy, you can move forward by finding the right foods to keep your mind—and body—on track.

This Is Your Brain at the Bakery

We may have hearts and spirits that science cannot explain, but at the most basic physical level, our human bodies are great melting pots of chemicals. So is every morsel of food we eat. Take a bite of anything, be it a banana or a cannoli, and your body breaks it down into chemicals that literally become part of you. The old cliché that you are what you eat is 100 percent true. That's why what you eat affects you so profoundly, not only around your waistline, but also above your neckline in your brain—altering how you think, feel, and react.

Think I'm exaggerating? Let me pull out a little science. In a study of 200 people, British researchers found that when the men and women limited the amount of sugar, caffeine, alcohol, and chocolate (notice they didn't make them *eliminate* any of these foods—more on that later) they ate and increased how much water, fruit, vegetables, and oil-rich fish they consumed, 88 percent of them said they felt happier, calmer, and more energetic. Twenty-four percent said they were less depressed, 26 percent had fewer mood swings, and 26 percent had fewer panic attacks and less anxiety. All from just changing how they ate!

And boy, do we as a culture need to change what we eat. When I look around New York—which is an active, walkable, fast-paced town—I see people getting heavier and unhealthier. Psychiatrists will tell you they're dishing out antidepressants like popcorn at Yankee Stadium. Little wonder we're so fat and depressed. The U.S. Department of Agriculture recently reported that Americans are eating *20 pounds more sugar and 35 extra pounds of white flour every year* than we did 30 years ago.

So what is it about those sweet, fatty foods that makes us feel so good and yet so bad at the same time? It all boils down to blood sugar. (Again, bear with me as I dig into some science; it's essential to understanding why what you eat so profoundly affects how you feel.) The main chemicals in your brain that control mood are called *neurotransmitters*, which include serotonin—Mother Nature's upper. Guess what fuels those mood-boosting neurotransmitters? You got it. Sugar. Now, Mother Nature is smart. She intended that we would graze on complex carbohydrates (which slowly break down to sugar during digestion) from whole grains, fruits, and vegetables to keep our blood sugar (and our moods) flowing nice and smooth and even all day. But we're always trying to mess with Mother Nature. So instead of eating whole oats or apples, we reach for cinnamon buns and chips and cookies—junk food that sends our blood sugar and serotonin levels skyrocketing. You get that killer food high for about 30 minutes. Then your body compensates by pulling your blood sugar back down, and your energy and mood crash like a train wreck, setting you up for another refined-carb binge like a junkie trolling for a fix.

Break the cycle by choosing your carbs carefully. When you're buying breads and starches, look for whole wheat and multigrain foods. Wholegrain carbs have more fiber, which slows digestion and keeps your energy and blood sugar levels even. If it doesn't have at least 2 grams of fiber per serving, put it back on the shelf. Even the most indulgent comfort food like mac 'n' cheese can be good for you and make you feel good if you make it with whole-grain pasta and low-fat cheese.

Finally, you need carbs for energy, so whatever you do, don't cut them out of your diet completely. Just be smart about where you get them. Pasta and bread aren't the only foods that contain carbs. You can get them from beans and lentils, sweet potatoes, and fruits and vegetables, which are also rich in other nutrients and phytochemicals (healing plant compounds) that help heal your muscles and keep you healthy. For ideas on smart carbs, check out my food recommendations later in this chapter.

What's Eating You?

You know the feeling. You've done nothing but sit at your desk all day, but you come home so wiped out you can barely budge, let alone get your butt to the gym. That's what stress does to you. We tend to think of stress as a physical phenomenon, something that just happens in our heads. But as I've said before, there's no line in the sand between your thoughts and your physical self; they're inextricably intertwined. Stress physically depletes you—a lot. When U.S. Department of Agriculture researchers studied the impact of a high-stress week on men and women eating a reasonably healthy diet, they found that blood and tissue levels of important vitamins and minerals dropped by as much as a third. If you do nothing to replenish those lost nutrients, your performance will suffer and your body will be vulnerable to sickness and infections.

The good news is that the Show It Love exercises will provide a healthy outlet for reducing your stress. But during high-stress times, be sure to pump your body full of the nutrients it needs to stay on top of the game. Here's what it needs most:

☙ **Antioxidants.** Stress produces cell-damaging molecules called *free radicals* in your body. Antioxidants like beta-carotene, vitamin C, and vitamin E are potent free-radical fighters. Beef up your patrols with fresh, brightly colored fruits and vegetables like strawberries, tropical fruit, dark green leafy vegetables, red bell peppers, carrots, sweet potatoes, and so on. The more colorful your food, the better it is for you.

∞ **B vitamins.** These nutrients fuel your nervous system, which revs into overdrive during high-stress times of your life. Deplete your B-vitamin stores and you'll end up feeling depressed, nervous, and plain run down. Fortified cereal and poultry are excellent sources of essential Bs.

∞ **Iron.** Iron is a critical part of your blood. It builds hemoglobin, which carries oxygen to your hardworking muscles. Run low and even the easiest treadmill workout will feel like the 20th mile in the Boston Marathon. Women lose iron every month during their period, and stress depletes it as well, so be sure you put plenty back with lean meat and fortified bread and cereal.

Go easy on sweets. Remember, that sugary doughnut may jack you up for a few minutes, but you'll ultimately end up feeling worse, and it delivers no nutrients—just fat, sugar, and white flour.

One final thought on stress eating. Oftentimes women don't just eat to boost their brain chemicals but also to have something to do so they won't think about what's really bugging them. (I'll admit, cheesecake can be a pleasant distraction.) Then when they (inevitably) gain weight, that's a distraction too. Think about it. How often do you blame the bad boyfriend and nowhere job on those 10 or 20 pounds you'd like to lose? I see this day in and day out. Women have this idea that if they could only lose weight, they'd have a perfect life. But they keep bingeing on bad food and piling on pounds so they never really have to face overcoming their fears or going for what they want in life. This I know: extra weight is almost always a symptom of unhappiness rather than the cause.

So next time you're standing in front of the fridge even though you're not at all hungry, try this exercise. Grab a pen and paper. Sit down (without any food) for 15 minutes. Without a plate of chips and salsa to dip and munch, your mind will be free—or more accurately, forced—to deal with what's really eating at you. Is it that extra project you agreed to take on at work even though you're already swamped? Did your girlfriends get together last weekend without inviting you? Has your mother been pining for the grand-kids she doesn't have yet (again)? Write down whatever comes to mind that's really gnawing at you. Then write down one action you'll take to make it better, and take steps to do it. Still hungry? I didn't think so. The more you take control of your life, the less you'll be trying to fill the void and shut down the stress with food.

Eating for Mental and Physical Vitality

As I explained earlier, you really are what you eat. So now that you're on the I Am part of your journey, really think about what you can eat to become the woman you want to be. If you want to be energetic and strong, you need to choose foods that will fill you with vitality, not bog you down. You also need to lay down a healthy foundation for the physical challenges coming up in I Can and I Do. The following is a guide to foods that can boost your mood as well as your physical performance. Some of them will undoubtedly surprise you.

Fat

Forget low-fat diets! You need fat and plenty of it! But not the burger-and-fries kind. You need the rich, heart-healthy, monounsaturated fat you get from olive oil, nuts, and avocadoes. Americans get hung up on counting every fat gram, while the people in Greece get 40 percent of their calories from fat yet have heart disease—and obesity—rates that are a fraction of ours. That's because Mediterranean countries know good fat! They eat a diet rich in fish and nuts, fruits and vegetables, and whole-grain breads and olive oil.

Studies show eating plenty of healthy fats like monounsaturated fats and omega-3 fatty acids from fish, nuts, seeds, and olive oil can keep your body running at its best for years to come, protecting you from heart disease, diabetes, arthritis, and breast cancer. Some doctors also believe that healthy fats give you beautiful, clear skin with fewer pimples and wrinkles. When I see a stunning, almost ageless woman here or abroad (especially in healthy fat–eating Mediterranean countries like Italy, France, Egypt, and Greece), I know she's eating right.

Healthy fats are also good for your head. While pizza and burgers and other saturated fat–filled foods physically reduce blood and oxygen flow to your brain, fogging up your concentration and making you less alert, foods rich in omega-3 fatty acids, like salmon, help rid the brain of cell-damaging free radicals. Studies show omega-3 fatty acids may also help raise serotonin levels and fend off depression.

Protein

Amino acids found in protein are your body's building blocks. It uses them to repair muscle tissue and manufacture the white blood cells that fuel your immune system. As your physical workouts become more intense, you'll need to stay on top of your protein consumption, so your muscles can quickly recover, rebuild, and be ready for the next go-round.

Mentally, protein helps keep you alert. It increases the production of the neurotransmitters (brain chemicals) dopamine and norepinephrine, which are known for their mentally energizing effects. Since carbs tend to have the opposite effect (soothing you, rather than jazzing you up), some experts believe that when you sit down to a meal, you should eat your protein before your carbs. I don't know that you need to go that far, but for breakfast and lunch, when I need to be sharp for the rest of the day, I definitely try to lean more heavily on the protein and lighter on the carbs.

Finally, protein also helps keep you lean. High-protein foods like lean meats and legumes increase what's known as *satiety*, which is just a fancy way of saying they help keep your blood sugar even and leave you feeling satisfied longer, so you don't get hunger pangs and start searching for a Snickers bar an hour after you eat.

Before you load up on beef jerky, however, know that I do not advocate any trendy super-high-protein or ultra-low-carb diets. You need carbohydrates to fuel your workouts as well as protein to repair your muscles. That means eating a smart, balanced diet that includes both. How much protein is enough? Active women need about 80 grams a day. A 4-ounce serving of chicken breast delivers about a third of that, so you don't need any special protein bars or shakes; it's easy to get all that you need through diet alone.

Chocolate

What would life be without it? So many of my clients go straight to Doctor Godiva to get through PMS, and considering all the feel-good chemicals chocolate contains, it's no wonder. Chocolate is like a psychoactive cocktail of feel-good brain chemicals, including tryptophan, phenylethylamine, and theobromine, and the end result is like a soothing amphetamine. You're calm but ready to roll. Maybe that's why the Aztecs swore by hot, frothy chocolate as a restorative stimulant and why warriors, nobility, and priests throughout the ages have hailed its nearly medicinal powers. Not surprisingly, chocolate is also one of the original Goddess foods. Fermented hot chocolate was a sacred beverage associated with Xochiquetzal, the goddess of fertility.

I urge my clients not to feel guilty about chocolate. Guilt only leads to hiding and bingeing and shame. You don't need any of that in your life. Especially since chocolate is good for your spirit, mind, *and* body. A chunk of rich, dark chocolate is brimming with the same heart-healthy flavonoids as red wine. In fact, in one recent study, scientists found that people who eat a little dark chocolate every day actually have more flexible, better-functioning arteries than those who don't.

Of course, just because chocolate is practically nectar from the gods, you don't have carte blanche to dive into a bag of Dove chocolates with abandon. But I do believe that a healthy, daily indulgence can be just what you need to keep from feeling deprived and to prevent junk-food binges. If you love chocolate, by all means have it. Buy the good stuff—the darker the better—and allow yourself about an ounce a day.

Fruits and Vegetables

Want to know one of my favorite "diet" tips? Every time you sit down to a meal, draw an imaginary line down the center of your plate, and fill one half with fruits and/or vegetables. Then divide the other half into quarters. Put meat or another protein source on one quarter and your starchy carbohydrate (like potatoes or pasta) on the other quarter. Bam! You've created the perfect meal with just enough protein, carbs, and plant foods. If you're still hungry when you're done, you can serve up seconds on the veggie/fruit side. It's the easiest way I know to keep your portions in check without measuring and counting calories, and it guarantees you get all the healthy antioxidants and healing plant compounds you need to keep your mind and body strong.

If you're like most Americans, who struggle to eat a measly three servings of fruits and vegetables a day, this might be the toughest advice yet. But it's also the most important. Remember (and repeat it over and over to yourself), you are what you eat, and there is nothing healthier, stronger, and more natural than food that comes straight from the rich, fertile soil of the earth. Nothing. Fruits and vegetables are the real staff of life. Every single day scientists are discovering compounds in plant foods they didn't even know existed that fight cancer, heart disease, Alzheimer's, and other debilitating illnesses. The antioxidants in fruits and vegetables help mend your muscles and speed your recovery so you can train harder and come back faster, ready for more. Finally, I have yet to meet anyone who ever got fat from eating too many blueberries or too much broccoli.

Seeds and Nuts

Seeds and nuts are a rich source of essential vitamins and minerals, including selenium, potassium, vitamin E, magnesium, folate, and more. Though they're high in fat, it's the healthy kind, so it's actually good for your heart. In two landmark studies involving tens of thousands of men and women, researchers found that people who ate nuts two or three times a week lowered their risk of heart disease by 35 to 47 percent compared to those who rarely ate them.

I like them because they're a natural, healthy, filling snack. A handful of mixed nuts and seeds, like almonds, walnuts, sunflower seeds, and Brazil nuts, satisfies your hunger much longer than some empty, nutritionally barren snack like popcorn or pretzels, and it's 100 times better for feeding your active body's nutritional needs.

Because every nut and seed has a different nutritional profile, you can get the most out of them by buying a mixed bag, like trail mix. Nuts and seeds are high in calories, though, so pour out a handful and put the bag back on the shelf. If you have trouble digesting seeds and nuts, you can substitute with nut butters. Be sure you choose natural varieties and, again, eat only small amounts because of the high fat and calorie counts.

Eat Early

The trick to keeping your metabolism set on high throughout the day is to eat three square meals and two light snacks. Of all those meals, none is more important than breakfast. Yet this is the one so many women skip. Listen. After seven or eight hours of sleep, your liver glycogen stores (carbohydrates that provide energy) are down 80 percent. You're literally running on fumes. By skipping breakfast, you start the day out in starvation mode and end up with less energy to tackle the mental and physical challenges that await. Women who forgo their morning meal are also more likely to overeat at dinner. That's probably why studies show that breakfast-skippers are four and a half times more likely to be obese than those who start the day with a healthy meal. The ideal breakfast contains some healthy whole-grain carbs, protein (like a hard-boiled egg), and a piece of fruit. Wash it down with some water and coffee, and your metabolic pump is primed.

Forgive (and Maybe Cleanse) Yourself

Even the most centered, well-intentioned woman occasionally blows it—sometimes for days on end. It's just part of life. Last year around the holidays, I went to one party after another until I didn't want to see a fatty hors d'oeuvre or sweet cocktail ever again. It's not that I don't know better or that I'm some sort of party girl. There were just a lot of wonderful people doing a lot of wonderful socializing, and I got caught up in the hoopla. But even with all the indulging, I never once thought, "Wow, I really blew it," because I didn't.

You are what you do 365 days a year, not a few weekends in December. If you're good to your body most of the time, you can go off course occasionally and still get right back on track. Which is exactly what I do. Because if you sit there and beat yourself up and tell yourself you're worthless and have no willpower, you're setting yourself up to make those occasional indulgences a daily occurrence, and that's where women get into trouble.

My advice for one or two bad days is simple. When you wake up with that food hangover, look in the mirror and say, "Hey, I'm human. I had a little too much fun yesterday. But today's a new day, and I'm right back on track." Then give yourself a smile and move on. If you've careened off track for weeks on end, it can be harder to break the cycle. That's when I turn to a deep body cleanse.

I believe in the balance of yin and yang. A few days of too many potato chips can be straightened out with a few of clean eating. Two weeks of ice cream and pastries? That requires more drastic measures to get back in balance. That's why I like the Master Cleanse.

The Master Cleanse (based on Stanley Burroughs's book *The Master Cleanser*) is a purifying drink you use as part of a fast. It helps eliminate toxins and acts as a tonic for the organs that handle the body's waste—the kidneys, liver, and digestive tract. The recipe is simple:

- ∞ 2 teaspoons lemon or lime juice (half a lemon or lime)
- ∞ 2 teaspoons pure grade B maple syrup
- ∞ Cayenne (red) pepper to taste
- ∞ 12 ounces cold purified water

You can double the ingredients and fill a thermos to sip from all day. Unlike a plain water fast that can leave you feeling tired and headachy, the ingredients in the Master Cleanse are energizing, so you can do it for a couple of days or more and feel fantastic. It is best to do a fast with Master Cleanse for at least four days. If you want, you can drink plain water in addition to the Master Cleanse drink. When I feel really bogged down during the holidays or after a vacation, I know I can use the Master Cleanse to bring my body back into balance quickly and easily.

"Try Something New Already" Food Recommendations

Like most women, you've been up and down your grocery store's aisles so many times you could probably shop for your staples blindfolded. But if you're going to change your eating habits, you'll have to change your shopping habits first. That means turning off autopilot and trying a new navigation system. Consider this list your copilot. I'm not going to tell you every last item to buy but rather guide you in making some healthy choices.

My biggest tip: when you get to the grocery store, shop around the entire perimeter before you start walking the aisles. The edges of the store are where the freshest foods—like produce, meat, fish, and dairy—are kept. You want to fill your cart with those before you add your canned, frozen, and packaged goods. Here are some selections I swear by.

Produce

Pick up the usual—baby carrots, asparagus, broccoli, berries of all kinds, citrus fruits, and so on. Then be sure you grab these:

- **Endive.** Endive leaves are perfect "scoopers" for tuna and chicken salad. Load them up for a healthy, crunchy wrap instead of bread or crackers.
- **Prewashed, bagged greens.** Spinach, arugula, collard greens, and so on. Heat some olive oil in a pan and sauté the greens for 2 minutes. They're absolutely delicious and perfectly nutritious.
- **Broccoli rabe.** It now comes prewashed and bagged.
- **Asian pear.** Perhaps the perfect fruit, it's juicy, firm, and crisp. It's also bursting with flavor and filled with fiber, so it's enormously satisfying.

Meat/Deli/Fish

Choose nitrate-free lunch meats like honey turkey. They don't last as long, but they'll keep you eating fresh. I also enjoy lean meat, poultry, and fish. My favorite is salmon, the healthiest fish you can eat. I serve it up sashimi-style: sliced thin; drizzled with olive oil; and sprinkled with pepper, sliced scallions, and a little salt. It's the best snack, lunch, or quick meal I know.

Dairy

Pick up your staples, like skim milk and eggs, and add in a little soy milk for variety. Next, be sure to toss these in your cart:

- **Good cheese.** Slapping tons of cheese on everything is guaranteed to widen your butt. But a little bit of the good stuff satisfies body, soul, and most definitely taste buds. Try rich, flavorful cheese like Asiago, Gruyère, and Scamorza.
- **Yogurt.** One of nature's perfect foods, it contains good bacteria that keeps your digestive tract healthy, and it goes with everything. I mix it with fruit for breakfast, nuts for lunch, and curry for dinner.

Canned Foods

I eat fresh when I can, but there are hectic, crazy times when I crack open my cupboards and thank my lucky stars for canned food! Canned beans (including refried beans) and canned tomatoes help create quick meals. Here's what I always have on hand:

- **Crab.** It's great on a salad, in a spread, or stuffed in salmon or cod; I eat it plain or flavored with curry, pepper, or other spices.
- **Tuna (light).** Everyone adds mayo, but if you use a little olive oil, pepper, and spices, you don't need it. If you like the creamy taste, try a spoonful of plain yogurt.
- **Chicken.** This is a new discovery for me, and I'm loving it. It's a quick, tasty way to pump protein into your salads and wraps.

Frozen Goods

Frozen vegetables are as nutritious as fresh and obviously more readily available year-round. If you have trouble finding fresh produce where you live, take a trip down the freezer aisle. And while you're there, be sure to pick up a bag or two of edamame, my favorite snack! These sweet, nutty soybeans are sold frozen in the pod. You just boil them in some lightly salted water and then flavor them with anything you like—cayenne, garlic, ginger, whatever strikes your fancy. They're a great source of soy protein.

Cereals/Pasta/Grains

High-fiber cereal is a mainstay of my morning meals. I pour a bowl, add some blackberries, and I'm ready to rock. Other good grains for lunch and dinner include brown rice and whole wheat pasta, though I have to say I'm not a big starch fan, since pasta and rice tend to deliver a lot of carbs and calories without many vitamins and minerals. During the cool months when I want some heavy comfort foods, I turn to potatoes, especially these:

- **Sweet potatoes.** These antioxidant powerhouses top almost every nutritionist's list of superfoods. I like mine roasted with a little cinnamon and ginger.
- **Purple fingerling potatoes.** Nutty and filling, they pack the same potent antioxidant that gives blueberries their rich violet hue. They're also slightly less starchy than white potatoes, so they help you maintain more even blood sugar levels.
- **Red potatoes.** When I can't find purple potatoes, I grab small red potatoes to roast with rosemary. They're naturally sweet and, like purple potatoes, less starchy than the white ones.

Bread

As with starchy grains, I try to go easy on bread, and I make my selections wisely. Any bread you choose should be whole grain and contain 3 grams of fiber per slice. The same goes for muffins and rolls. For a great bread substitute, I buy Wasa Crispbread. A crisp, crunchy hybrid of bread and crackers, Wasa bread is ideal for lunch. It has only 32 calories per slice yet delivers 2.5 grams of fiber, as well as a healthy dose of protein and essential minerals like magnesium.

Condiments

Broaden your horizons past ketchup, mayo, and mustard. Most of these are loaded with sugar and fat. You want something that'll kick up the flavor of your food without weighing it down. I love these:

- **Chili sauce.** Mix it with fruit (like cranberry sauce) for an exotic hot-sweet sensation that makes any meat mouthwatering.
- **Chutney.** Forget drawn butter! Spicy, fruity, savory chutney is the way to go for shrimp and seafood.
- **Hummus.** Use it as a spread in place of mayo on sandwiches.
- **Salsa.** It's better on burgers than ketchup.

Spices and Herbs

I believe food should have "flava"! When a meal is intricately spiced, you eat more slowly to savor each bite, and you're less likely to overdo it because you're eating at a healthy pace and both your stomach and taste buds are satisfied with less. Experiment with what you find in the spice aisle. I like to blend a few. (Try garlic powder and cayenne with a pinch of salt, and coat foods before sautéing. Delish!!) Here are a few of my favorites:

Cayenne pepper
Coarse salt (sea salt)
Curry powder
Garlic powder
Onion powder
Rosemary
Thyme

Control Cravings

Food cravings are your body's way of telling you what it needs—emotionally and physically. It's important not to ignore them. But it's equally important not to give in every time that little voice calls out for potato chips. Often, it's just asking for something out of force of habit. For instance, if you always eat chocolate chip cookies when you're sad and bored, that's what your body will come to expect. If you take a second to decipher the craving and give your body a healthier alternative, over time it will start asking for those foods instead. The chart that follows lists some smart substitutions for your most common cravings.

IF YOU CRAVE THIS	YOU WANT THIS	SO EAT THIS
Ice cream	A cool creamy concoction of sugar and fat to soothe your nerves	My City Girl Trifle (p. 36)— a sweet, smooth blend of berries and yogurt
Potato chips	Something salty, fatty, and crunchy; a snack that makes your mouth work and takes your mind off the day's worries	Spiced nuts, like a teriyaki trail mix. You'll get a savory crunch with healthy fat.
Pizza	A cheesy, chewy, substantial snack—something to fill an emotional and a physical need	Whole-grain pita pizza. Slice a whole-grain pita in half, spread a little marinara sauce on it, and sprinkle with some mozzarella. Toast it until the cheese melts. All the good stuff without all the grease.
Peanut butter crackers	Something smooth and substantial (Your body may need protein.)	Get your protein and peanut butter fix without the refined carbs of crackers or white bread. Slather a couple of teaspoons of peanut butter on apple slices or celery sticks.
Chocolate	Chocolate	Chocolate. Seriously! As discussed earlier, chocolate is a special craving that can be fulfilled only by the real thing. The key is not to eat some cheap, milk chocolate candy bar but to feed your body with the good (dark, rich) stuff.
Cookies	Something crunchy and sweet that takes you to a simple, happy place	Granola bars (the old-fashioned crunchy kind, not the less healthy chewy ones). They've got a cookie quality but are lower in calories and a good source of protein and fiber. You can also try a small, whole-grain muffin.
Soda	Something fizzy and sweet to boost your spirits and tickle your tongue	Ice-cold mineral water with a splash of crancherry or other sweet juice

Simple Dishes That Satisfy

Eating well doesn't have to be a production. In fact, it shouldn't be if you expect to do it day in and day out. Here are some of my favorite toss-together dishes that keep me going strong.

City Girl Trifle

½ cup fat-free Cool Whip

½ cup low-fat or fat-free yogurt (plain or flavored)

¼ cup reduced-fat sour cream

1 banana, sliced

¼ cup sliced strawberries

¼ cup blueberries

Combine Cool Whip, yogurt, and sour cream in a bowl, and mix until smooth.

In a large, clear bowl or small parfait dish, create uniform layers of the individual fruits followed by the cream, and keep building. Your finished dish will be pretty to look at and delicious to eat.

1 serving

NUTRITION FACTS PER SERVING: **CALORIES** 370; **FAT** 10 g (saturated, 6.1 g; polyunsaturated, 0.3 g; monounsaturated, 0.6 g); **PROTEIN** 11.1 g; **CARBOHYDRATES** 60 g; **FIBER** 4.8 g; **CHOLESTEROL** 38 mg; **IRON** 1 mg; **SODIUM** 144 mg; **CALCIUM** 339 mg

Kacy's Energy Mix

1 cup dry-roasted, unsalted almonds

1 cup dried cranberries

Combine the two ingredients in a resealable plastic bag. This quick and easy snack will kill your midday hunger cravings while giving your metabolism a quick boost.

8 servings (serving size = ¼ cup)

NUTRITION FACTS PER SERVING: **CALORIES** 148; **FAT** 9.1 g (saturated, 0.7 g; polyunsaturated, 2.2 g; monounsaturated, 5.8 g); **PROTEIN** 3.8 g; **CARBOHYDRATES** 15.8 g; **FIBER** 2.8 g; **CHOLESTEROL** 0 mg; **IRON** 1 mg; **SODIUM** 0 mg; **CALCIUM** 46 mg

Turkey Wasa Sunshine

6 ounces whole-berry
cranberry sauce

¼ cup low-sodium
cranberry chutney

6 Wasa Light Rye
Crispbread slices

½ pound of nitrate-free,
deli-sliced turkey breast

6 romaine lettuce leaves (or
your green of choice)

In a medium-sized bowl, combine cranberry sauce and
chutney; mix well.

Spread each Wasa crisp with 2 tablespoons of the
cranberry sauce/chutney mixture. Place about a slice of
turkey on each crisp, followed by a romaine lettuce leaf,
and you have yourself a quick, light, tasty meal.

2 servings

NUTRITION FACTS PER SERVING: **CALORIES** 395; **FAT** 3.1 g (saturated, 0.04 g;
polyunsaturated, 0.14 g; monounsaturated, 0.04 g); **PROTEIN** 24.5 g; **CARBOHYDRATES**
67.1 g; **FIBER** 6.9 g; **CHOLESTEROL** 40 mg; **IRON** 3.3 mg; **SODIUM** 1,120 mg; **CALCIUM**
98 mg

Spicy Edamame

1 bag frozen edamame
(soybeans)

¼ teaspoon cayenne pepper

½ teaspoon sea salt
(optional)

Follow cooking instructions on the edamame package;
combine with the other ingredients while the edamame
is still warm. This Asian delicacy is light, full of vitamins,
and packed with protein. The added cayenne pepper
gives this dish a little extra kick.

2 servings (serving size = ¾ cup)

NUTRITION FACTS PER SERVING: **CALORIES** 150; **FAT** 4.5 g; **PROTEIN** 12 g;
CARBOHYDRATES 13.6 g; **FIBER** 6 g; **CHOLESTEROL** 0 mg; **IRON** 7 mg; **SODIUM** 423 mg;
CALCIUM 75 mg

Smoked Salmon Carpaccio

4 ounces sliced smoked salmon

1 tablespoon fresh lemon juice

1 clove garlic, finely chopped

1 tablespoon olive oil

¼ cup chopped green onion

Fresh ground black pepper to taste

3 Wasa Light Rye Crispbread slices

1 cup mixed green salad

Arrange salmon slices on a platter so they are close but not overlapping. Cover with plastic wrap and refrigerate until needed.

Place lemon juice and garlic in a small bowl, and beat with a fork. Slowly beat in the olive oil. Add half of the chopped green onion to the dressing mixture, and reserve the rest.

Drizzle the dressing over the salmon slices and garnish with the remaining green onion. Grind black pepper to taste over salmon. Serve with Wasa crisps and salad, and enjoy!

1 serving

NUTRITION FACTS PER SERVING: **CALORIES** 371; **FAT** 19 g (saturated, 3.0 g; polyunsaturated, 2.8 g; monounsaturated, 12.2 g); **PROTEIN** 24.4 g; **CARBOHYDRATES** 26.9 g; **FIBER** 6.2 g; **CHOLESTEROL** 26 mg; **IRON** 3 mg; **SODIUM** 975 mg; **CALCIUM** 76 mg

Hibiscus and Green Tea with Lemon

1 bag hibiscus tea

1 bag green tea

1 lemon wedge or
1 teaspoon lemon juice

Boil 2 cups of water. Pour into your favorite teapot, add tea bags, and steep for 5 minutes. Finish with a squeeze of lemon. This hot beverage is loaded with vitamin C as well as antioxidants.

1 serving

NUTRITION FACTS PER SERVING: **CALORIES** 1.3; **FAT** 0 g; **PROTEIN** 0 g; **CARBOHYDRATES** 0.4 g; **FIBER** 0 g; **CHOLESTEROL** 0 mg; **IRON** 0 mg; **SODIUM** 0 mg; **CALCIUM** 0.4 mg

3

Woman Warrior Series 1

Feel the Power from Within

The mind-body connection is undeniably strong. How you feel about your body affects how you move, and the way you move your body can profoundly affect how you feel. Case in point: Italian-born supermodel Greta Cavazzoni has entered her 30s still smokin' hot. Her body is as good, if not better, than it was when I started working with her in her 20s. Most important, she's centered. She can eat, enjoy her life, and still be ready when the cameras start clicking. That's because she's not blocked with self-hatred. She knows she has to honor herself on an emotional, spiritual, and physical level to stay in the game.

She also knows that sometimes movement is the first step to opening up and purging yourself when your life is out of whack. I remember a few years back, she walked into the studio and started going through this series of exercises. Immediately, I could see the turmoil bubbling to the surface.

I put my hand on her shoulder and said, "Greta?" She just broke down and the tears fell. After talking and crying it out, she finished her workout, getting more bold and beautiful with each move. With every lunge and leg lift, she forged a deeper connection with her inner warrior and released the pain that was dragging her down. A short while later, she let go of a bad relationship. She continues to embody the wonders of Show It Love.

In this chapter, you'll find the first Woman Warrior exercise series—my recipe for washing away the hate. The grace and strength of these moves force you to reach deep down and pull out not just your inner goddess but also that bad bitch you've been holding down for too long—the one who can reclaim your personal power and space. Especially for women who are unhappy with their lower-body area, this series is like my secret weapon. These moves zone in on your hips, thighs, and butt and make you feel the raw power in all those places you hate. They also yield results quickly for an added emotional boost.

Are You Feelin' It?

Before you start exercising, it's important to make a mind-body connection, to develop a strong sense of body awareness and really *feel* the muscles that are performing the exercise. Too often women (and men) move mechanically through their workouts. They're going through the motions all right, but they aren't concentrating fully. They aren't zeroing in on the muscles they're trying to activate or pouring all their physical and mental efforts into their workouts. That level of attention is critical if you want to tone, shape, and firm stubborn areas in your hips, thighs, and butt.

Remember, what you think literally affects how your body responds. Every single muscle fiber in your arms, legs, belly, back, and butt is wired to your brain. When you go to curl a dumbbell, your brain sends out a signal to fire your biceps muscles into action so you can lift the weight. But your body has wisdom, and it uses only as many muscle fibers as absolutely necessary to perform the work, so you always have some energy to spare. That was great for our ancestors, who labored in the fields all day and then had to have the strength to fend off animals or warring tribes. But when you're trying to shape, strengthen, and tone your body, you want every possible muscle fiber working! And that takes concentration.

To see what I mean, try this: Let your right arm hang down by your side. Now touch your right shoulder with your right hand. Your biceps muscles barely budged, right? Try it again. Only this time, pretend you're holding a brick in your right hand. Mentally focus on contracting your biceps muscles as hard as you can, and squeeze your muscles tight as you slowly curl your hand to your shoulder. Feel the difference? So many of my clients come in thinking they have to hit the weights hard and lift gargantuan loads to make gains. But nothing could be further from the truth. In fact, science shows that if you consciously forge powerful mind-muscle connections, you can get stronger without even lifting a finger.

It's true. Researchers from the Cleveland Clinic Foundation recently reported that the mind is so powerful that the mere act of *thinking* about lifting weights can make you stronger. Check this out: The scientists gave 30 men and women strength tests and then divided them into three groups. For 15 minutes a day, five days a week, group one imagined exercising just their pinkies, visualizing moving all the muscles in the finger and making it stronger; group two imagined doing the same thing with their biceps, and group three did no imaginary exercise. After 12 weeks, the finger exercisers improved their pinkie strength by 53 percent; the biceps group boosted their arm strength by 13.4 percent; and (not surprisingly) the nonvisualizers made no gains. When your brain forges a connection with your muscles, they respond by getting ready for action whether or not you actually move them. And when you do, watch out! That's why I designed the Woman Warrior exercises to squeeze every last muscle fiber to fatigue. You'll challenge your arms, legs, and core from every angle, and most important, you'll move mindfully, mentally firing and activating all your muscles as you go through the moves.

In the end, it's all about treating your muscles with the attention and respect they deserve. Be present for your body as you flow through this series of exercises. Stand tall. Move strong. Keep your muscles fired from start to end. Act as though I'm right there in your living room watching your every move. Make it purposeful. Make it pretty. Before long you'll be feeling—and showing—a little bit of warrior goddess edge all the time, whether you're sitting at your desk or strutting down the street.

Get in Gear

You can do every single move in this book without setting foot in a gym. Obviously, I don't have anything against health clubs and gyms; I've worked in one almost all my life. But I know plenty of women feel uncomfortable in those mirrored rooms full of men or find health clubs too inconvenient or expensive. That's okay. With about $100 worth of equipment, you can transform your body without ever leaving your living room.

Here's what you'll need:

- **Comfortable, stylish clothes and good shoes.** Remember, Show It Love is about feeling good about yourself. So toss aside those ratty sweats, the body-hiding, tentlike giant tees, and all the stuff you wouldn't even walk out to get the mail in, and break out something a little more stylish. Your workout clothes should be body-skimming enough that you can watch your form and see your muscles move but also loose enough to bend and reach comfortably.

Many Show It Love strength moves are explosive, and the cardio plans that are coming up in the next chapter are energetic and fast-paced. So don't try busting these new moves in those old tennis shoes. Invest in a pair of well-cushioned, supportive athletic shoes like cross trainers or running shoes. Do your feet a favor and buy them from a specialty shoe store instead of a department store. The staff at the specialty store will measure your feet; check the height of your arches; and watch how you stand, walk, and run before recommending a shoe that is the best biomechanical fit for you. You'll be amazed how much lighter and more agile you'll feel in a quality pair of shoes.

∞ **A staff.** Nothing makes you feel more like kicking some ass than wielding a big stick! I perform many of my Woman Warrior exercises using a large 5- to 6-foot wooden dowel (you can buy one at most home improvement or hardware stores). But any broomstick or light body bar (9 to 12 pounds max) will work just as well, provided you can get a nice wide grip on it.

∞ **A body bar.** For some moves, you need more weight than a dowel can provide. For the best results, pick up a dowel and a heavier body bar (about 18 pounds). Or, as mentioned above, you can buy a light body bar to stand in for the dowel and a heavier one for the exercises that require more resistance. Body bars are available nearly everywhere, including sporting goods stores and big-box retailers. Or you can find them online at bodybar.com.

∞ **Hand weights.** Invest in two sets of dumbbells: a light pair (3, 5, or 8 pounds) for working your shoulders and a medium pair (10, 12, or 15 pounds) for working the larger arm muscles, your biceps and triceps. I also like using an 8-pound medicine ball for some of the moves, but it isn't necessary. You can hold a dumbbell with two hands instead.

∞ **A mat.** If you're not working on a lightly carpeted floor, have a mat handy for the floor work to protect your back. If you don't have a mat, a folded thick towel will do.

The I Am Woman Warrior Moves: Body-Love Power

"Holy shit! I can't believe I just did that!" That's what women almost always say after our first training session together. They come in full of self-doubt, and after a few sets and reps, they're brimming with pride. They're literally in awe of their own ability and can't believe they had the power and grace within them to perform these warrioresque moves. Sometimes they even get a little nauseous from digging deep into their physical reserves and reaching for and realizing their limits. That's okay. I love that they're opening up and working hard enough to need to sit down and regroup. Sometimes we need to get a little weak on our feet to get really, really strong and healthy. But there's a difference between discomfort and pain. Discomfort helps you grow. Pain is bad. You don't want to hurt yourself. So proper form and technique are very important.

Start with your breathing. Pull air into your lungs like you would fill a pitcher with water, filling the bottom first and working your way up to the top. Breathe in through your nose, drawing the air all the way into your diaphragm so your belly expands before your chest rises. Then exhale through your mouth. You'll breathe deeply and rhythmically just like that throughout these moves: inhaling to draw in strength and prepare to move, exhaling to help push your muscles through the exertion phase of the exercise.

Every move will start in the power position. Stand tall, keeping knees soft. Pull your navel to your spine and maintain a straight back and tight, firm belly. In this position, you're guaranteed not to sleepwalk through your exercise or, worse, fall into sloppy form. Each Woman Warrior series begins with a trio of core exercises that are designed to tap into your emotional, spiritual, and creative power center. Yes, they'll give you killer abs. But more important, they'll awaken your senses and prepare your body for the challenges that follow.

The Details

Reps. Each time you perform a move, it's called a repetition, or rep. Perform 12 reps of each move. For single leg moves, perform 12 reps per side for a total of 24. For lean, toned, beautiful muscles, I swear by using light to moderate weight (or sometimes body weight alone) and fatiguing the muscles through a full range of motion and high number of repetitions.

Sets. Each time you complete the designated number of reps for an exercise, it's one set. You should go for three sets right away. If you can only do two, try lowering the weight. Concentrate on feeling your muscles and perfecting your form.

The weight. The weight you choose should be heavy enough so that the final three reps of a set feel very challenging. As you get stronger, the moves will feel easier. When those last reps are no longer kicking your ass, it's time to pick up heavier weights.

Progression. For the first week, perform the routine in traditional strength training fashion, completing all three sets of each exercise before moving on to the next one. Starting with week two, perform the moves as a circuit, completing one set of each move, then immediately moving to the next exercise, completing the entire sequence a total of three times. Every time you increase your weights, go back to traditional, three-sets-in-a-row lifting for one week before again performing the routine as a circuit.

Times per week. You will be performing the Woman Warrior exercises three days a week, along with I Am cardio exercises three days a week. See the I Am Workout Log on page 94 for your complete I Am exercise program.

Movement prep. Before starting, do five minutes of light cardio exercise, like jumping jacks or running in place, to warm up your muscles and get them ready for action.

Stand in the power position, with your feet wider than shoulder-width apart and slightly turned out. Hold your arms out to the sides, palms facing forward.

THE MOVE: Show Some Love

YOU'LL FEEL IT: In your abs, back, chest, hips, and glutes.

THE BODY-LOVE BENEFIT: It warms up your entire core, loosens up your spine, and relieves tightness in your hips and pelvis. You'll feel an awakening in your creative center and the rising power in your glutes and thighs.

Contract your pelvis and abdominals, pushing through your hips and bending your knees slightly, bringing your pelvis toward your ribs. At the same time, pull your arms together in front of your body with your palms facing up, and drop your head forward. Really squeeze your abs, glutes, and chest at the end of the move. Hold for 1 second.

Open back up past the starting position, pushing your butt back, opening your arms wide, and arching your back slightly. Repeat the entire motion for the full set.

KACY'S COACHING TIPS: This is a warm-up movement, so take the first few reps to stretch out and loosen up your muscles. Then really get into it, thrusting that pelvis like a traditional African dancer (this is where showgirls get their swing). Put a little "pop" in it. Have some fun, and feel your body move.

Lie on your back with your arms extended overhead, palms facing each other. Bend your knees and place your feet flat on the floor, hip-width apart.

THE MOVE: Fire in the Belly

YOU'LL FEEL IT: From your breasts to your hips. Unlike most ab curls and crunches, which are done slowly, this move taps into your deepest muscle fibers to propel your torso off the floor. Your entire abdominal area will be giving a shout.

THE BODY-LOVE BENEFIT: Your belly is where you create and feel life. This exercise develops its strength all the way to your center. Strong abs also help you stand straight and tall, giving you a formidable presence.

In one explosive move, contract your abs and curl your head and shoulders off the floor, sweeping your arms over your head and down to your sides, with your hands reaching toward your feet and palms facing your thighs. Hold for a count of 4. Slowly release back to the starting position.

KACY'S COACHING TIPS: Keep your movements controlled. You shouldn't be flopping up and down off the floor like a fish out of water. Burst up quickly and powerfully. Hold in the curl position with your body completely quiet. Then ease back to the floor, staying in control.

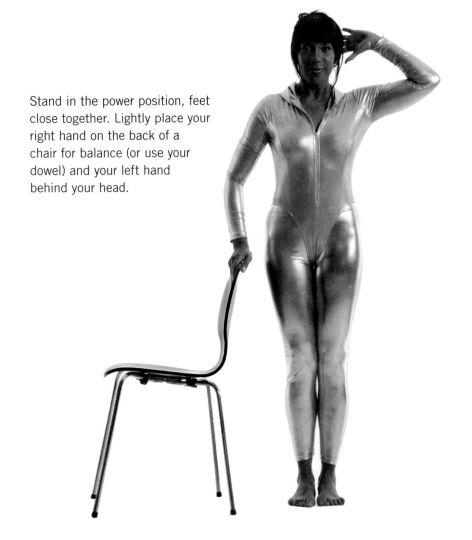

Stand in the power position, feet close together. Lightly place your right hand on the back of a chair for balance (or use your dowel) and your left hand behind your head.

THE MOVE: Side Bow

YOU'LL FEEL IT: Through your core and in your hips, glutes, and outer thighs. You should also feel a nice stretch through your sides.

THE BODY-LOVE BENEFIT: This is a very powerful but graceful move that hones your balance and stability. The rhythmic, dancelike quality of it will bring out your feminine energy.

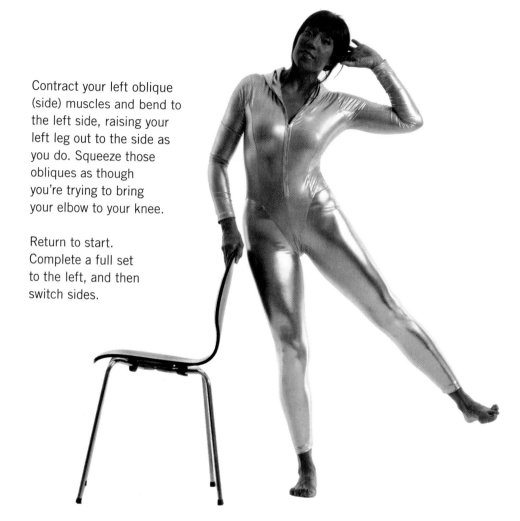

Contract your left oblique (side) muscles and bend to the left side, raising your left leg out to the side as you do. Squeeze those obliques as though you're trying to bring your elbow to your knee.

Return to start. Complete a full set to the left, and then switch sides.

KACY'S COACHING TIPS: Try to keep your balance rock solid while performing this move. Squeeze your glutes and keep your abs tight throughout the exercise to prevent unwanted swaying or twisting. As you get more comfortable and confident, try doing it without holding on to anything.

Stand in the power position, feet slightly apart. Place your left hand on your hip. Hold a staff or body bar in your right hand for support. The end of the bar should be positioned close to the toes of your right foot. Lift your right leg so it's bent at a 90-degree angle and your knee is even with your hip.

THE MOVE: Warrior I

YOU'LL FEEL IT: Immediately activating every muscle fiber in your hips, thighs, and glutes.

THE BODY-LOVE BENEFIT: From supermodels like Iman to the soccer mom off the street, every woman loves this exercise because she feels a warm, satisfying burn inside the hardest-to-reach lower-body trouble spots. Master this move, and you'll be ready to conquer the world.

Swing your right leg back into a deep lunge position, so that it is bent as close to 90 degrees as possible, with the ball of your foot on the ground (heel lifted). Your left leg should form a 90-degree angle, with your left knee directly over your ankle.

Return to the starting position but don't pause. Immediately flow into the next rep in a fluid motion. Complete a full set without pausing, and then switch sides.

KACY'S COACHING TIPS: Avoid leaning heavily or pushing on the body bar during the move. Keep your grip light, and use the bar for balance only. Maintain the movement using your lower body.

Stand in the power position, with your feet close together, heels touching and toes turned out. Place your hands on your waist and tighten your abdominal muscles.

THE MOVE: Duke Curtsy

YOU'LL FEEL IT: Right where you want it most, in that impossible-to-target "saddlebag" area, where your outer thigh meets the side of your booty.

THE BODY-LOVE BENEFIT: Feeling this area burn and work is incredibly empowering. You finally feel something positive happening in the very place that has held so many negative feelings for so, so long. Embracing this area is a giant step toward real body love.

In a single fluid movement, bring your right leg behind and to your left, bending both knees into a curtsy while keeping your back straight.

Return to the starting position. Complete a set, and then switch sides.

KACY'S COACHING TIPS: Perform this one with grace and strength, as though you were dropping to the floor in front of the queen herself, but never bow or bend forward; keep your back straight. Be sure to complete the full range of motion, taking a great big step back and dropping all the way to the floor.

Stand with your feet wider than shoulder-width apart and turned out at 45 degrees—like second position in ballet. Place your hands on your hips. Bend your legs so you're almost in a squat, but keep your back straight and don't stick your butt out.

THE MOVE: Plié Drag

YOU'LL FEEL IT: In your butt and inner thighs.

THE BODY-LOVE BENEFIT: The inner thigh is another underused and much reviled body part. Women rarely participate in activities that allow them to feel the power of these muscles. Strengthening the thighs from every angle improves your power and stability.

Shift your balance to your left leg and drag your right foot along the ground toward your left, so that your heels come together as you straighten your legs.

You should feel this in your inner thighs. If you don't, press more weight into your right foot as you drag. Repeat with the left leg.

KACY'S COACHING TIPS: Because most women don't engage in much side-to-side activity, as in tennis and basketball, they often have weak inner thighs. Pretend you're squeezing an exercise ball between your knees to fully engage these muscles. Try moving a little faster each time you bring your legs together to really fire up those inner thigh muscles.

Stand in the power position, feet shoulder-width apart. Hold a weighted body bar down in front of you, palms facing your thighs.

THE MOVE: Flip, Squat, Press

YOU'LL FEEL IT: In your booty, thighs, hips, arms, shoulders, and upper back.

THE BODY-LOVE BENEFIT: Gravity, combined with all the time we spend parked on our behinds, brings our booty down. This butt-blasting move puts a little lift back in your Levi's by firming your backside and creating a sexy separation between your butt and the back of your legs. It also puts power and presence in your shoulders, arms, and upper back.

Bend your elbows and flip the bar up to your collarbone while you simultaneously squat back as though sitting in a chair until your thighs are parallel to the floor.

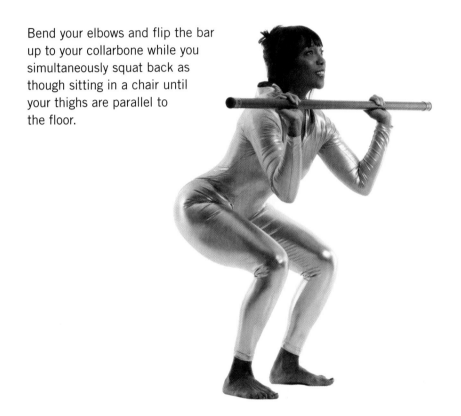

continued »

KACY'S COACHING TIPS: This is a power move that uses every muscle in your body, but make it look pretty by keeping it fluid and graceful. Watch that your knees don't jut out too far over your toes in the down position to keep your hinges healthy and safe.

Press back up to a standing position, immediately pressing the bar over your head.

Lower the bar, and repeat the entire sequence.

THE MOVE: Flip, Squat, Press, *continued*

Assume a squat position with your legs bent about 45 degrees. Hold a light dumbbell in each hand, arms bent so the weights are positioned just in front of your chest, palms facing each other.

THE MOVE: Push, Pull, Kickback

continued »

YOU'LL FEEL IT: In your chest, back, shoulders, and triceps. You'll also get a bonus burn in your thighs and booty from performing this exercise in the squat position.

THE BODY-LOVE BENEFIT: As you develop and harness the raw power in your chest and back, you won't need help hauling home your latest flea market finds, and you'll carry yourself with more confidence.

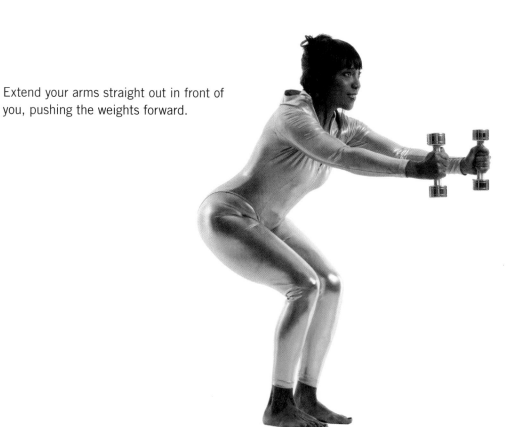

Extend your arms straight out in front of you, pushing the weights forward.

THE MOVE: Push, Pull, Kickback, *continued*

KACY'S COACHING TIPS: It's a good idea to try this one without any weights to start. Engage your chest, back, and triceps through the full range of motion. That way when you do add weight, you'll be sure to engage all the right muscles to do the work.

Then bend your elbows, squeeze your shoulder blades together, and pull the weights back to either side of your chest.

Finally, straighten your arms out behind you.

Stand in the power position with your feet close together, knees soft. Hold a dumbbell in each hand, elbows bent so forearms are straight out in front of you at waist level, palms facing up. (You can instead hold a weighted body bar, if you prefer).

THE MOVE: Serve It Up

YOU'LL FEEL IT: In your chest, biceps, and shoulders.

THE BODY-LOVE BENEFIT: This move gives your chest a nice boost. No, you can't "train" your breasts. But by firming up the tissue beneath them, you can give those B or C cups a nudge in the right direction.

Squeeze your biceps, and while extending your arms raise the weights straight up in front of you until they reach just above chest height, as though you were holding up an offering. Your may naturally bend your knees and tilt your head up slightly for balance as you perform this move.

Lower back to the starting position.

KACY'S COACHING TIPS: This is an upper-body exercise, so be sure to keep your lower body as quiet as possible. If you have to hoist your hips or sway your back to get the weights up, they're too heavy.

Stand in the power position, feet close together, knees slightly bent. Hold dumbbells in your hands with your arms extended straight down at your sides, palms facing your thighs.

THE MOVE: Open with Purpose

YOU'LL FEEL IT: In your shoulders, back, and chest.

THE BODY-LOVE BENEFIT: Strong, curvy shoulders are like the creamy froth on your cappuccino—a smooth balance to the bold strength below. In my experience, women who feel good about baring their arms embrace the world with greater ease.

Keeping your arms extended, raise them straight out in front of your body until they are parallel to the floor.

continued »

KACY'S COACHING TIPS: Remember to initiate the opening and closing of your arms with the big muscles in your back and chest, not just your shoulders. This move is meant to tone your entire upper body.

Next, squeeze your shoulder blades together and open your arms straight out to the sides, so your body forms a T.

Squeeze your chest, and bring the weights together in front of your chest. Lower them back to the starting position.

THE MOVE: Open with Purpose, *continued*

Stretch It Out

I'm going to tell you straight up, flexibility is the first thing to go. Your muscles and connective tissue lose some of their natural elasticity over time, especially if, like most women, you spend 8 to 12 hours a day parked at a desk, behind a steering wheel, on a subway, and/or crashed out on the couch. As muscles become shortened and tight, you're more vulnerable to aches, pains, and injuries. It's also harder to exercise properly and get the most from your workouts if you can't move your joints through their full range of motion.

But that's likely old news. Everyone knows that tight muscles make it harder to exercise and move your body with strength and confidence. What you may not have thought of is how stiff muscles and rigid joints make you feel. If your hamstrings and back are all wound tight, how can you dance at a party or bounce down the street on a beautiful, clear day? If your hips are rigid and inflexible, how can you be fully sexual and enjoy yourself in bed? If your shoulders are locked up and your neck is hunched forward, how can you see the world for all it has to offer and be open to new experiences, both physical and emotional? You can't. Stretching may be a good idea to keep your muscles healthy and limber, but most important, it opens you up to living life to your fullest capacity.

The Show It Love exercises are designed to lengthen as well as strengthen your muscles by challenging your arms, legs, hips, and core through their complete range of motion. But I believe you should set aside a few minutes each day to stretch. A good stretch boosts circulation, lubricates your joints, and "wrings" metabolic waste out of your muscles. And it feels so damn good! Like strength training, it can help you connect with and appreciate your body on a whole new level. Here are five flexibility exercises that will help open your body, heart, and soul.

Perform these moves slowly, gracefully, and purposefully. Perform each stretch three times, trying to move a little deeper into the positions each time. I recommend doing these moves right after you wrap up your I Am strength and cardio workouts when your muscles are warm and pliable.

Sit tall with legs crossed and back straight. Hold your dowel overhead, hands slightly wider than shoulder-width apart. Keep your shoulders down and relaxed.

THE STRETCH: Swaying in the Breeze

YOU'LL FEEL IT: From your waistline straight to your arms, as well as from your lower back up through your spine to your shoulders. Offers an added bonus of a great abdominal stretch.

With your back straight and long, bend
to the left as far as is comfortable
(slide your hands along the dowel
if it touches the floor). Hold the
position and breathe deeply
for 5 seconds.

Return to center, and then
repeat the stretch to the
right. Return to center.

continued »

THE BODY-LOVE BENEFIT: This upper-body stretch lubricates the spinal column and
increases the blood flow to your body and brain.

Finally, drop your arms forward and lean back slightly, curving your upper back and dropping your head. Hold for 5 seconds.

Return to the starting position, and repeat two more times.

THE STRETCH: Swaying in the Breeze, *continued*

Sit tall with legs crossed and back straight. Hold the dowel straight out in front of you at chest level, hands slightly wider than shoulder-width apart. With your back straight and long, rotate to the left as far as is comfortable. Hold and breathe deeply for 5 seconds.

Return to center, and then repeat the stretch to the right.

Return to start, and repeat two more times.

THE STRETCH: Seated Twist

YOU'LL FEEL IT: In your full abdominal wall, including your obliques. You'll get an extra stretch in your chest, shoulders, and upper and lower back.

THE BODY-LOVE BENEFIT: This stretch will prepare your abdominals for action or thank them for working hard. Either way they'll shout, "I'm alive!"

Stand tall with your feet hip-width apart, holding the dowel down in front of you, arms extended, palms facing thighs. Step your right foot forward, planting the heel on the floor, foot flexed, and bend your left knee, sitting back in a semisquat. Keeping your back straight, press the dowel straight out and down toward your right toes, feeling the stretch down the back of your right leg. Hold 10 seconds.

THE STRETCH: Bend and Extend

YOU'LL FEEL IT: From the backs of your thighs (hamstrings) right to your butt (the glutes), with a hip-flexor and upper-back stretch thrown in as the finishing touches.

THE BODY-LOVE BENEFIT: This stretch is the after-dinner mint for your hamstrings and glutes; it leaves them feeling happy and fresh.

Switch the dowel to your right hand and place one end on the floor by your right foot. Roll onto your right foot and bend forward from the hips, while lifting and extending your left leg behind you until your body forms a T. Allow your right knee to bend naturally, and reach to touch the floor with your left hand for balance, if needed. Hold for 5 to 10 seconds.

Return to a standing position. Repeat with the left leg, and then do the whole sequence two more times.

Stand tall, holding the dowel in your left hand with arm extended and one end of the dowel planted on the floor in front of you. Cross your left ankle over the top of your right knee, so your left knee is pointing out to the side. Using the dowel for balance, bend your right leg and sit back as far as is comfortable, feeling the stretch deep in your hips and glutes. Hold for 5 to 10 seconds.

Return to a standing position. Repeat with the opposite leg, and then do the whole sequence two more times.

THE STRETCH: Figure 4 Sit-Back

YOU'LL FEEL IT: Deep in your hips and glutes.

THE BODY-LOVE BENEFIT: This easy "ahhh" stretch is a direct target to the butt and hips. It's a great way to show some booty love.

Stand tall, holding the dowel in your right hand with one end planted on the floor to the outside of your right toes. Take a giant step back with your right leg, bending the left knee 90 degrees and planting the right knee on the floor. Keeping your back straight, press your pelvis forward, feeling the stretch through the front of your hips. Hold for 5 to 10 seconds.

THE STRETCH: Deep Hip Drop

continued »

YOU'LL FEEL IT: Through your hip flexors and thighs.

THE BODY-LOVE BENEFIT: This stretch brings out the warrior goddess in all of us. It says, "I have worked hard, I have conquered, I have arrived!"

Next, press back to a standing position, bend your right knee, and reach back and grasp the top of your right foot in your left hand. Gently pull the foot toward your butt, feeling the stretch through your thigh. Hold for 5 seconds.

Return to starting position, and repeat to the opposite side.

THE STRETCH: Deep Hip Drop, *continued*

How's It Going?

The first thing every woman does to measure her progress is jump on the scale. But I have news for you: the scale may not budge for a while, and it's got nothing to do with whether or not you're making progress. As you start strength training and building lean muscle, you're bound to get more svelte, but depending on your body composition, you may not lose weight.

Let me explain. Muscle tissue—the stuff that makes you look lean and shapely—takes up about half as much space as fat, but it weighs about twice as much. When you start performing your Warrior exercises and doing the Show It Love cardio routines, you'll be burning off fat, but you'll also be gaining muscle. So while your hips, thighs, belly, and booty are losing inches, the needle on the scale may not waver more than a few ticks. Don't sweat it! In fact, stay away from it. There's more to measuring progress than the numbers on a scale. Here are a few of my favorites:

- **Pants check.** Take out your favorite pair of pants that you no longer wear because they're too tight. When they no longer ride up your butt and give you a wedgie, you've slimmed your hips and thighs by a few inches. How your clothing fits is the best indication of how effective your workouts are.
- **Muscle squeeze.** Touch yourself. Seriously, take your hands and feel your biceps and triceps. Feel your thighs and butt. Can you see sexy muscles starting to peek through? Are they getting firmer? With this hands-on approach, you can literally feel how well the program is working.
- **Talk test.** Losing inches and body fat is great, but maybe the most important measurement of your progress at this stage is how you talk to yourself. Are you still talking trash about your booty and belly? What thoughts run through your head as you look in the mirror? If you're making real progress, those thoughts and feelings should be turning more positive. If they're not, you should be working on your mirror exercises with the same intensity you use with the strength training and cardio routines. Remember, your body follows your mind, so you have to make progress there first. (Check out the I Am Milestones on page 92 for a full measure of your body-love progress.)

4

Move That Beautiful Body

When a client is stuck in a body rut, one of the first things I check is her cardio routine. What I usually find is that she is joylessly stomping through the same old routine on the StairMaster. Your heart is a very special, important muscle. It is the engine that pumps your life force throughout your body. As it gets stronger, so do you. Show it some love with joyful, energetic movement. You'll be rewarded with a better body and a stronger spirit.

The first step is to realize that routine exercises that let you "zone out"—watching television or just letting your mind wander to what you're going to have for dinner or what's going on at work—are *not* the way to go. Give your body complete non-attention and you won't see much progress. Instead, concentrate on varying your routine and doing cardio exercise that forces you to be *completely in the moment*. This doesn't mean dropping the StairMaster forever. Just vary your routine so much that your body sees each exercise as a new mountain to climb, a new challenge to overcome. As with my clients, my goal here is to send you down the right path. But my hope is that you'll take this knowledge and—literally—run with it, creating your own energizing cardio routines that will keep you moving strong and burning fat.

The Heart of the Matter

Most women do cardio to burn fat. That's a great side benefit, but first and foremost, a cardio workout is about honoring and empowering your most precious muscle: the heart. The average woman's heart beats about 75 times per minute—more than a beat per second—while she's just hanging around, doing the dishes, or watching TV. An active woman's heart, on the other hand, bumps out just 50 or 60 beats per minute. Do the math. That adds up to 36,000 fewer beats every single day, or 13 million fewer at the end of just one year. The easier it is for your heart to do its job, the longer it will last and the better you will feel.

That is the foundation of cardiovascular exercise—it makes it easier for your heart to do its job. Every time you push your heart out of its comfort zone, whether it's by cranking up the incline on the treadmill or banging out sprints on the exercise bike, your working muscles shout out to your heart that they need more oxygen and nutrients to keep you moving. Your heart starts thumping faster and harder to deliver the goods. Keep it up, and your heart responds like any muscle, by getting stronger. Your body makes other important adaptations too. More capillaries form in your muscles, so you can pour more nutrient-rich blood where you need it, and your cells' energy-producing furnaces get bigger, so they can use oxygen (and burn stored fat) faster to keep you cranking along. Over time, your heart can squeeze out more blood with every beat, and your body can use every ounce of that life force faster and more efficiently.

A strong, fit heart will give you the stamina to push yourself through your Woman Warrior exercises, taking your muscles to a level you didn't think possible. It will help you keep up with your kids, your job, and your house without feeling so run down. In the end, everything you do will feel easier. And when everything you do feels easier, you'll feel like doing more. That's why cardio exercise, though it uses lots of energy, leaves you feeling so energized. But again, barely breathing hard on the elliptical while leafing through the latest issue of *Cosmo* just isn't going to get the job done.

To strengthen your heart, you need to push it past its resting rate into a hardworking zone. How do you know if you're working hard enough? Take the "gab test." Here's how it works:

EXERTION LEVEL: Easy

- **Gab test:** At this level of exertion, you can chat to your girlfriend on the treadmill next to you with ease. You can dish out the blow-by-blow of last night's date in vivid detail, right down to the balsamic reduction on the seared honey-dipped scallops, all without stopping to take a breath.
- **What it's good for:** Warming up. It's important to take 3 to 5 minutes to slowly ramp up your heart rate, lubricate your joints, and warm your muscles before turning up your exertion. During the first minute or two of activity, you *should* be able to dish on last night's dessert without being breathless.
- **But watch out:** Don't turn gym time into social hour. Cardio should feel this easy only at the very beginning and very end of your workout.

EXERTION LEVEL: Moderate

- **Gab test:** You should be breathing a little too hard to give every juicy detail of the latest bit of office gossip, but you can still converse in short sentences like, "I hear there's a cute new guy in marketing." (Pause for a breath.) "And he's single."
- **What it's good for:** This is classic endurance training. It's a sustainable level of exertion for almost all exercisers, good for burning calories and building general heart strength.
- **But watch out:** It's easy to get stuck here because it's a comfort zone. But if you never push past it, your body will adapt to the exercise demands and you'll stop seeing benefits from your cardio sessions.

EXERTION LEVEL: Hard

- **Gab test:** You should be huffing and puffing in a controlled, rhythmic fashion. Any conversation is reduced to two- to three-word phrases like, "What's up?" and "Oh, same stuff."
- **What it's good for:** Boosting your aerobic capacity, or how hard you can go before your muscles start burning and force you to slow down. When you train in this tough zone, even for short stretches, your body gets that much better at using oxygen, so your "cruising speed" becomes faster. In other words, you naturally move faster (and burn more calories) without feeling like you're working harder.
- **But watch out:** Working out at this level is strong medicine, so you always want to give your body proper time to recover and regenerate.

EXERTION LEVEL: Defcon-5

- **Gab test:** Gab? Are you joking? You can barely grunt out a response.
- **What it's good for:** Everything! Pushing yourself to this top level for 20 or 30 seconds raises your fitness ceiling. And when you raise the top end of your fitness capability, everything else follows.
- **But watch out:** If you're brand-new to exercise, save this high-intensity work until you have six to eight weeks of training under your belt (no matter how quickly you progress through the stages of the Show It Love program). You may be fit enough to turn it up to 10, but your joints and connective tissue need time to get strong enough to push that hard without getting hurt.

Burning Fat—Fast

There are still women who are afraid to get their heart pumping hard because they believe that only low-intensity exercise burns fat. That old "fat-burning zone" myth just refuses to die!

Here's the real deal. Your body does use different sources of fuel during varying exercise intensities. Stored fat takes longer to convert to energy than stored carbs, so when you're just tooling along, barely breaking a sweat, your body has the time to tap into and burn up some of your fat stores. When you've got it revved up into the red, it burns mostly quick-burning carbs for fuel. But it never uses just one or the other, so what's really important is how many calories you burn. Hands down, running burns more calories than strolling, and if you do the math, you'll see it also burns more fat.

Check this out: When you exercise in the easy to moderate range, about 60 percent of the calories your body burns are from fat and 40 percent from carbs. About 35 percent of the calories burned during moderate to hard efforts are from fat and 65 percent from carbs. Let's say you walk briskly with easy to moderate effort for 30 minutes. You'll burn off about 130 calories. (This is based on activity for a 140-pound woman. Lighter women burn less, heavier women burn more.) Seventy-six of those calories are from fat. Now, let's say you crank it up to a jog for 30 minutes. This time you burn 320 calories, 111 from fat. The bottom line is you burn more calories, which is the only way to drop weight you don't want, *and* burn more fat by going faster. That's why all of my cardio routines, even those for the newest newbies, include a little kick in the ass. You get fitter faster and get more benefit for the time (and sometimes money) you invest.

I can hear you saying, "But Kacy, I hate to run!" or "I'm not fit enough to run!" Don't sweat it. Show It Love is about just that—showing yourself love. So I will not be forcing you to do a lot of stuff you hate. But I will make you work—even if it means tilting that treadmill toward the sky and hoofing it up a steep "hill" to get your heart rate banging and your fat stores frying. And I'll tell you what. Even if you're not jumping for joy while you're cranking out those high-energy intervals, you'll be beaming like the sun when you're done, because you'll have a sense of pride and accomplishment that you got it done and honored your body with some hard work.

Spread the Love

Your body was created to move, and I recommend that you get up and get it going at least 30 to 45 minutes a day most days a week. If you can't do it all at once, spread it out throughout the day. Really. No one says you have to do all 30 minutes of your cardio routine in a row for it to count. In fact, if you check out the latest research, the opposite is true. Spreading your exercise throughout the day may help you get fitter and burn fat slightly faster than doing it all in one fell swoop. In one recent study of nearly 60 women, researchers at the University of Pittsburgh found that those who sneaked in four 10-minute quickie cardio sessions a day most days a week dropped 20 pounds in 20 weeks—6 more pounds than the women who banged out 40 minutes a day all in one shot.

Why the big difference? Partly because the women who spread out their activity stuck to the program better, and in the end, they actually exercised more minutes a day than those who were told to get it all in at one time. Think about it. With work and kids, most of us don't have a huge chunk of free time during the day. But we've got plenty of 10-, 20-, or maybe 30-minute windows that we can fill with activity. Another advantage to quickie workouts is that if you plan on doing a little something in the morning, at lunch, and then in the evening, and you end up oversleeping or a meeting runs long and you miss one of those workout sessions, no big deal. You've still done two workouts. If you plan on hitting the gym once at 5:30 P.M. and a meeting runs long, your exercise plans for the day are DOA. And we all know something is a heck of a lot better than nothing.

Another bonus of spreading out your workouts is a big metabolism bump. After you work out, your heart rate and calorie burn stay elevated for up to an hour after you finish. So if you exercise two or three times throughout the day, you'll get a bigger afterburn effect than if you pump your heart rate up just once. That means you burn more calories with the same total exercise time. In the end what matters most, as Nike says, is that you just do it.

Bust a Move: Cardio Workouts

Your body is an amazingly adaptable machine. Throw it a challenge and after a few swings, it will knock it out of the park. That's good because it helps you master sports like golf and swimming and step up to big life challenges like carrying babies, hauling heavy loads, and everything else you have to do to survive. It's bad because when you're working out to get in shape, your body responds to the initial challenge by shedding fat and building muscle, but then it grows accustomed to the workload and you stop seeing those fast and furious results.

That's why Show It Love cardio is all about keeping your body guessing. Every time you lace up your workout shoes, your body should be thinking, "Oh shit, what's she going to throw at me this time?" The more you keep changing it up, the faster your results will come. Once you get the hang of it, you'll start coming up with your own inventive combinations and cardio challenges. In the meantime, here are some of my favorite ways to shake your body up, get it in shape, and show it some love in motion. These workouts will take 15 to 30 minutes. If you want to split them up into shorter segments, simply do half the workout and save the rest for later. Or shorten the interval times and do the whole routine. The choice is always yours.

NYC Body-Shaping Circuit

I'm a born and bred New Yorker. Though I have a nice apartment, it's still a New York apartment, so it's not like I have a garage to store a bunch of bulky equipment or a basement to spread out in. That's why I put together this time- and space-efficient NYC Body-Shaping Circuit. As long as you have about 10 feet of floor space, you can get your heart revved up anytime, anywhere. Here's how:

❧ Warm up with a minute or two of marching in place, swinging your arms and getting the blood flowing.

- Run in place for 30 seconds, bringing your knees as high as possible and pumping your arms vigorously.
- Rest for 10 seconds.
- Repeat five more times, alternating between 30 seconds of high-knee running and 10 seconds of rest.
- Perform 12 Jump Squat Thrusts (see page 174 for exercise description).
- Rest for 10 seconds.
- Repeat five more times, alternating between 12 Jump Squat Thrusts and 10 seconds of rest.
- Perform 30 seconds of Heel-Click Pliés, without weight (see page 222 for exercise description).
- Rest for 10 seconds.
- Repeat five more times, alternating between 30 seconds of Heel-Click Pliés and 10 seconds of rest.
- Cool down with a minute or two of marching in place, swinging your arms overhead and stretching as you slowly bring the routine to a close.

Lower-Body Treadmill Blast

Some women love to zone out on the treadmill. That's okay sometimes. But if you want to benefit yourself physically, you need to zone in once or twice a week and give your body full attention. This Lower-Body Treadmill Blast demands 100 percent effort and gives 100 percent rewards.

- Warm up with three to five minutes of walking at a comfortably brisk pace (3.5 to 3.8 miles per hour).
- Racewalk for two minutes. Increase the speed to 4.0 to 5.0 miles per hour. Don't run. Take short, quick strides, fully engaging your glutes and pumping your arms.
- Recover for two minutes at a brisk pace (3.5 to 3.8 miles per hour).
- Repeat racewalk/recover cycle two more times.
- Run for two minutes. Increase the speed to 5.5 to 7.0 miles per hour. Jog or run, so you're breathing hard. This should rank as hard on the gab test scale.

- Recover for two minutes at a brisk pace (3.5 to 3.8 miles per hour).
- Repeat run/walk cycle two more times.
- Cool down at an easy pace (less than 3.0 miles per hour) for one to two minutes.

Hiking the Himalayas

Ever see a mountain climber with a fat butt? Me either. That's why I love this high-tilt treadmill workout. It shapes your butt and thighs as though you were trekking up the Grand Teton. It's also great for body-love. Women who climb will tell you that you simply can't hate a pair of thighs that gets you to the top of a mountain. Enough said.

- Warm up with three to five minutes of walking at a comfortably brisk pace (3.5 to 3.8 miles per hour) with the treadmill set on 0 degree of incline.
- Increase the incline to 4 percent. Walk for two minutes. Keep your hands off the console and rails; swing your arms; and take long, strong strides.
- Decrease the incline to 1 to 2 percent, and recover for two minutes.
- Increase the incline to 6 percent. Walk for two minutes. Again, keep your hands off the console and rails; swing your arms; and take long, strong strides.
- Decrease the incline to 1 to 2 percent, and recover for two minutes.
- Increase the incline to 8 percent. Walk for two minutes. Touch the console lightly with your fingertips if needed for balance, but try to keep your arms swinging and your strides strong and long.
- Decrease the incline to 1 to 2 percent, and recover for two minutes.
- Increase the incline to 10 percent. Walk for two minutes. Hold on lightly as needed. Stride with high knees, as though you're climbing up a hillside.
- Increase the incline to 12 percent for one more minute, cresting the mountain. Give it all you've got!
- Decrease the incline to 1 to 2 percent, and recover for two to three minutes.

To Thineself Be True

There are as many ways to get cardiovascular exercise as there are ways to move your body, so expand your horizons. Look for opportunities to move your body whenever you can. Not sure where to start? I find that most clients have a certain "fitness personality." They are (not surprisingly) attracted to activities that jive with who they are. It sounds like common sense, but most of us don't think of fitness that way. Here are seven of the most common fitness personalities I see. Which one are you?

Fitness Personality: Social

Telling traits: Few things bring you more joy than a booked social calendar. As long as you're dashing off to dinners here and outings there, you're a happy camper.

Try: Book exercise classes. Every gym has a roster of classes a mile long with a little something for everyone. You can belly dance, kickbox, ride bikes—you name it. The class regulars become like old friends, and pretty soon you'll have an even wider social circle to go out with. Even if you don't belong to a gym, most towns have a community center or adult education classes where you can sign up by the class.

Fitness Personality: Competitive

Telling traits: Even if it's a game of Go Fish with your four-year-old nephew, you *really* want to win. You feel challenged if you see someone running at a faster pace on the treadmill next to yours.

Try: Join a league. From lacrosse to field hockey, there's an adult league battling it out every night of the week. If you're not a team-sport person, sign up for a 5K race or a triathlon.

Fitness Personality: Inquisitive

Telling traits: You're the one on the museum tour asking all the questions while the rest of the group is mindlessly nodding along. If there's something to learn, you're there.

Try: DVDs—lots of 'em. The nice thing about DVDs is that most come with many layers of explicit instruction. You can learn all kinds of new workouts, all without leaving your living room.

Fitness Personality: Meditative

Telling traits: You look inward more than outward, preferring to take the time to reflect and think before you speak. You crave all things peaceful, from steaming cups of tea to flickering candles.

Try: Yoga is obvious, but to get your heart rate up while centering your spirit, try repetitive-motion sports like swimming, jogging, cycling, kayaking, or rowing. Studies show that the repetitive movements in these sports can put your brain in a Zen-like state.

Fitness Personality: Outdoorsy

Telling traits: You live in your L.L. Bean gear and always carry a backpack. You'd rather run in the rain than resort to the treadmill. If there's a mountain, lake, ocean, or trail to explore somewhere, you're there.

Try: Hook up with a hiking, cycling, walking, or running club. A group of outdoorsy kindred spirits will introduce you to new places and gear and provide a community for swapping stories.

Fitness Personality: Romantic

Telling traits: You like journaling, scrapbooking, decoupaging, and antiquing. Chances are you care how your body looks, but you're not all that interested in traditional exercise.

Try: Dancing. There is nothing more romantic than dance, be it flamenco, salsa, ballroom, African, or even line dancing. You get to dress up and move to your favorite music.

Fitness Personality: Type A

Telling traits: You want results—preferably in 20 minutes or less, because, damn it, you have three meetings and a haircut this afternoon. You really don't care why it works, just that it does.

Try: Interval training. The three workouts in this chapter are the perfect launching pad. Once you've mastered them, move on to the routines in I Can and so on. By the time you get to I Do, you'll be mixing and matching your own routines. Just be careful. As much as you may like to, you shouldn't do intervals every single day. Your body needs the chance to rebuild to get stronger and fitter without just breaking down.

I Am Milestones

Are You Ready for the Next Step?

When is it time to leave I Am behind and move on to the next section of the book? Body love can't be timed; it may take you a day or a month to heal your relationship with the butt and belly that have carried you through your life. The Show It Love program is based on love, and love does not have a timetable or a deadline. You're ready to move on to the next section of the book when you can look at yourself in the mirror without being bombarded by negative thoughts, when you feel your power and strength rising with every Woman Warrior lunge, and when you see food as nourishment and celebration rather than therapy and punishment.

The following questionnaire will help you measure your progress. You should move on to I Can when, deep in your heart, you can answer the following questions positively and truthfully:

1 **Walk past a mirror and catch a look at yourself. What was your first impression?**
   a. My eyes zoomed to my flaws.
   b. I appraised myself objectively and saw progress in my body.
   c. I immediately thought something very positive like, "Way to go, girl!"

2 **When you last saw a good friend, which best describes your actions at the time?**
   a. I obsessed about how much nicer her legs/butt/thighs are than mine.
   b. I asked her about her workouts and compared notes.
   c. I didn't think much about my body or hers.

3 When you do your mirror work, appraising and talking to your body, which of the following do you do?

   a. I continue to feel self-conscious and embarrassed.

   b. I giggle a little but otherwise get to it.

   c. I feel a strong sense of self and self-acceptance.

4 How would you describe your current relationship with food?

   a. It's the one thing I haven't been able to deal with or change.

   b. I'm not perfect, but when I slip, I get back to business without remorse or excessive self-punishment.

   c. I've made a big commitment to healthier eating.

5 During times of high stress, what is the first thing you do to find peace?

   a. Dig into a bag of chips or pint of ice cream.

   b. Sometimes I reach for sweets or snacks, but I am more aware of my eating habits and try to limit my portions and make healthier choices.

   c. I indulge in a small square of chocolate, then I take a deep breath and repeat some of my empowering self-affirmations until I feel centered again.

6 How does exercising make you feel?

   a. Self-conscious.

   b. Ultimately strong and wonderful, but I still struggle with being positive and present while I work out.

   c. Like I'm queen of the world!

If your answers are mostly c, then go right ahead to I Can. If your answers are mostly b, move on but continue to work in the I Am exercises every couple of days. If, however, in your heart of hearts, you're stuck at a answers, don't proceed yet. I Am is a powerful series that can lead to concrete change—don't rush it, but keep on at it. The transformation will come, and when it does, there will be no stopping your forward progress!

I Am Workout Log

Once you get in a groove with your workouts, they'll feel like second nature. But it takes at least 30 days to form a habit, maybe more if you're new to exercise. Keeping a log helps you make—and keep—your exercise commitments.

Your first week of I Am should look like this:

MONDAY	TUESDAY	WEDNESDAY	THURSDAY	FRIDAY	SATURDAY	SUNDAY
Woman Warrior, 3 sets Stretches	Cardio (e.g., Hiking the Himalayas, p. 89), 30–40 minutes	Woman Warrior, 3 sets Stretches	Cardio (e.g., Lower-Body Treadmill Blast, p. 88), 30–40 minutes	Woman Warrior, 3 sets Stretches	Cardio (e.g., NYC Body-Shaping Circuit, p. 87), 30–40 minutes	Off

Use the log sheet on the next page to track your progress.

I Am Log Sheet

THE MOVE	NUMBER OF SETS/ NUMBER OF REPS	I FELT . . .
Show Some Love	_____	_____
Fire in the Belly	_____	_____
Side Bow	_____	_____
Warrior I	_____	_____
Duke Curtsy	_____	_____
Plié Drag	_____	_____
Flip, Squat, Press	_____	_____
Push, Pull, Kickback	_____	_____
Serve It Up	_____	_____
Open with Purpose	_____	_____

THE CARDIO	NUMBER OF MINUTES	I FELT . . .
NYC Body-Shaping Circuit	_____	_____
Lower-Body Treadmill Blast	_____	_____
Hiking the Himalayas	_____	_____
Other _____	_____	_____

PART 2

I Can

THERE are no limits to what you can do when you believe in yourself. Unfortunately, confidence is a quality that too many women sorely lack. When faced with a great challenge, some women immediately respond, "I can't." But you really *can*. Now that you've explored your emotional relationship with your body and done some healing—so you're on a sound emotional footing—you can let your spirit soar.

Look, I know the obstacles you face. It is common knowledge that more than half of women who start an exercise program throw in the towel before six months is through. That's a reality I see in the club every single day. I believe that's because (1) they didn't start with a strong emotional foundation, which you've thoroughly addressed throughout I Am; and (2) they don't believe in themselves, so they make excuses and lose motivation. That's where I Can, step 2 of my program, comes in. Society has put so many restraints on women's thinking that they can't let their expectations fly. In I Can, I'll show you the potential and strength contained in your body and, more important, your spirit.

The I Can phase of your journey emphasizes setting unrealistic (yes, unrealistic) goals and denying excuses. In this section, physical activity, eating, and rest and recovery become joyful, spiritual exercises—the means to reaching your potential. You'll also find the second Woman Warrior exercise series, which promotes motivation in the form of spiritual empowerment achieved through increasingly challenging movement.

I designed the I Can sequence of strengthening exercises and cardio routines specially to reveal just what a woman's body can do, no matter what her body shape or fitness level is. Through graceful, powerful movement, I reveal the possibilities and invite women to seize them. We work to stretch the spine, feel the energy of the chest, and use the legs in new ways that reveal their potential and power. Spiritually emboldened, you will discover that exercise isn't some mechanical set of movements you sleepwalk through just to get it done; it's the act of screaming, "I am alive!" And equally important, in this part of my program, you'll learn how to joyfully feed your active body and nourish your soul.

Ultimately, the I Can section of Show It Love is a realization of self that will keep you going even through the toughest of times. Most important, by the time you turn the last page of this section, you will be your own life's motivation. You won't need people pushing you or outside intervention.

Excuses will be a thing of the past. You'll be exercising and taking care of yourself, by yourself and for yourself. You'll set your goals high and believe deep down inside that you can really, truly reach them.

Within the next few chapters, you will find:

- **I Can motivation tools.** Throughout this section, I'll teach you how to conquer your inhibitions and tap into your potential. You'll find an entire chapter on goals that will encourage you to really go for the body you've always wanted, and goal-setting sheets to keep you on track. I've also devoted a chapter to barriers and excuses. When you really want something, you find a way. Excuses are just hidden insecurities. You'll find self-analysis tools to dig deep into your psyche so you can discover—and do away with—what's really holding you back.

- **Soul food.** Every time you put a morsel of food in your mouth you are nourishing your spirit as well as your body. Though crème brûlée is one way to feed your soul, it's not the only one. The spirit of the I Can food section is learning how to experiment with colors and textures, flavors and spices, to give you a food high without weighing you down with lots of fat and calories. Because so many of us eat out and on the run these days, you'll find a special section devoted to making fast, healthy dishes at home.

- **Woman Warrior series 2.** I Can includes the second Warrior exercise series, which pushes you out of your comfort zone and unlocks your physical ability. The I Can cardio workouts serve as a complement to these strengthening moves, keeping your body from ever being bored while revealing your true potential. You'll also learn how to sit back, relax, and let all that hard work sink in. Time and time again you will amaze yourself with what you are able to do and how your body responds. If you never thought you could have sculpted shoulders or tight, toned thighs, be prepared to be surprised. By the time you leave this section, you'll never doubt your body's ability again.

Turn the page and get ready to say, "I can!"

5

Goal Setting

Be Unrealistic

I saw a new client the other day, a very successful photographer named Pamela, who had just turned 50. Pamela has worked with the most beautiful people in the world, capturing the most amazing bodies on film. She came to me unhappy with the softening and widening of her own body as she moved through menopause. The first words out of her mouth were, "Look, I'm not trying to be unrealistic . . ." I stopped her right there and said, "Maybe it's time to *be* unrealistic."

Sometimes it seems that no matter where we go in life, we are told to be "realistic." But to me, that's simply code for "Don't expect great things." Well, if you're not going to expect great things, what's the point in working hard? Sure, when you turn 40 or 50, you will see some effects of gravity. We all do. But if you're always looking down, letting the changes of time wear on you and trying to be "realistic," then the body you see will be much droopier, much heavier than it actually is. If you stand up, roll your shoulders back, and pull your navel to your spine, you'll see that you've been concealing the shape and strength of your body. You'll see grace and power within you. And that grace and power can help you achieve "unrealistic" goals.

Think about it. As you get older, you get wiser. You realize that life is an adventure and sometimes you just have to lay it all out there and go for it.

So why not take the same approach with your physical self? I train so many 40- and 50-year-olds who have bodies that are the envy of the 20-year-olds in the club. Why? Because they realize that they don't have to be put out to pasture at any age. They have made a conscious decision to think unrealistically and to go for the body they've always wanted. They've acknowledged that they may have let their physical selves slide over the years when they were busy with marriage and kids and career. But they also recognize that they have the power to reclaim their physical selves—to take back their power and grace, to look amazing, and to achieve a measure of fitness that surpasses the capabilities of their former 18-year-old selves. If you don't dig in and go for it now, when will you?

As for Pamela, after just one session, she went from, "I'm just being realistic," to "Wow, I didn't realize how much strength I really had in this body. I can't wait for our next session!"

What Is It You *Really* Want?

During the I Am phase of our journey, we worked on setting love goals, which are designed to take your focus off the typical, overly negative, physical goals ("I hate my big butt and I want it gone") to the internal goals ("I want to be strong and capable"). At no point do I want you to lose sight of those goals, because they are your essential foundation. But as we continue building, growing, and developing from the inside out, it's perfectly okay to look in the mirror and think, "I really would like a little definition in my arms."

So here's your chance. What are your pie-in-the-sky dreams? We'll take this section and set what I call your "glamour goals"—those body dreams you would realize if everything in your life went just the way you wanted it. We all have them; we want Beyoncé's booty or Hilary Swank's abs. Though these types of body wishes can be destructive if you make them your sole focus, if you handle them correctly, they can help you finally achieve the body of your dreams.

The deal is this: Most of the time your glamour goals are focused on areas of your body that have brought you some sort of unhappiness, maybe throughout much of your life. By doing the mirror exercises and affirmations in I Am, you should have shed your hatred of those areas (if you haven't, go back and keep working at it until you do, because nothing positive comes out of hate). You should now appreciate those body parts and feel the strength in them starting to grow. But you may still not completely love how they look in your favorite jeans. Hang tight. You'll get there.

Before we go any further, however, I'll be 100 percent honest with you. You may never reach your glamour goal. (That's actually the point, so follow me through.) Most celebrities are pretty busy with their own body parts, so no matter how badly you want Angelina Jolie's legs, you're not going to get them. And if you're 5'3" and she's 5'10"—well, you do the math. You can't stretch your bones. But you *can* get toned thighs and a firm rear that make you go, "Whoa! Check me out," when you slip them into a short skirt. And *that* is the ultimate goal of I Can. It's a spiritual transformation that takes you from always looking outward for motivation and affirmation to looking straight at yourself. You and you alone become your motivation. You will become so happy with your own arms, butt, and thighs that you'll stop wishing for someone else's. But it's perfectly okay if you got that inspirational ball rolling while flipping through the pages of *People* magazine.

So let's take a look at those glamour goals and see what it is you really want.

1 First, write down your glamour goal(s), such as "I want a butt like Halle Berry's."

_____

_____

2 List the reasons why you chose those goals, such as "It's firm and round; it doesn't jiggle when she walks."

_____

_____

3 Change the wording of your original goal to make it "me-oriented." The focus should now be on your body part(s) only, as in "I want my butt to be firm, high, and strong. I want it to look like I feel—powerful."

_____

_____

4 Finally, put those wants and wishes into a strong I Can voice. These are the "unrealistic" goals that you can and will make happen, such as "I can get a firm, toned butt that carries me through life and makes me proud."

_____

_____

Repeat these goals to yourself before each workout, but especially before you do your Woman Warrior exercises. Every time you lunge, squat, walk, and run, remind yourself what you're working for. If you're serious and ready for a positive change, you can make it happen. Every day that you wake up and say, "I can!" takes you a little bit closer to making your goals a reality.

"Oh, I Could Never . . ."

My cowriter, Selene Yeager, told me an interesting story while we were working on this book. Though she's a strong, competitive athlete today, she didn't think of herself that way 10 years ago. In fact, she was envious of her "brave" friends who lined up to do triathlons on sunny summer weekends. Then one Saturday morning at a women's sports conference, she was talking to one of the speakers, an Ironman triathlete. The woman asked Selene if she raced. Selene said, "Oh, no! I'd love to try a triathlon, but I could never do the swim." The woman gave her a look and said, "Girl, with shoulders like that, you could swim in your sleep. Sign up and jump in the water!" That's all it took. The next day Selene looked online for a local race, and four months of lap swimming, cycling, and running later, she was standing on the starting line of her first tri. Today, she's raced in events across the country and even qualified for some national championship events. All because somebody gave her belief in herself.

Now it's your turn. I believe in you, and you should too. If you are reading this book, you have what it takes to dig deep and make those kinds of dreams come true. Trust me. Thousands, if not millions, of regular everyday women of all ages, shapes, and sizes run, walk, bike, and shuffle their way through 5Ks, 10Ks, charity bike rides, and triathlons every year. There is no reason you can't. After you establish your glamour goals, I want you to take 5 to 10 minutes to start thinking about yourself in an athletic sense (this will pave the way for complete transformation in I Do). What athletic endeavors pique your interest or make you go, "Hmmm," before you proceed to dismiss them as impossible for you? Running a marathon? Climbing a mountain? Think hard about what would really thrill you and what you would be proud to accomplish.

I encourage all my clients to have one goal that is larger than their physical selves, because, believe it or not, even if you were to wake up tomorrow with Madonna's arms and Eva Longoria's hips and thighs, you still wouldn't be 100 percent satisfied. Real satisfaction comes from body love (I Am), believing in yourself (I Can), and achievement (I Do). Believing you can get a great derriere is fabulous, and working hard and achieving an aesthetically pleasing body is very satisfying, don't get me wrong. But the stuff you draw on when times are hard and what makes you feel really good about your body deep down inside are the things you have done with it.

Write down whatever comes to mind and circle the one option that excites you most. Now, let's take steps toward making that dream a reality.

1 First, write down your goal, such as "I want to do one of the all-women's triathlons, like Danskin's."

_____

_____

2 Write down what has stopped you from going for it in the past, such as "I don't swim very well. I don't know where to ride my bike to train. I'm afraid of making a fool of myself."

_____

_____

3 After each "obstacle," write a solution, or what you would have to do to overcome that barrier (this is good practice for blasting down barriers in your work and home life too). You might say, "I can take swim lessons at the Y. I can inquire about safe riding routes at the local bike shop as well as take a Spinning class to condition my body for cycling. I can attend a local triathlon or running event to check out the scene and assure myself that not everyone who participates is a skinny, ultrafit competitive type."

_____

_____

_____

4 Finally, write a concrete action plan for just one of those solutions, such as "I will enroll in the upcoming eight-week session of adult swim lessons at the local rec center." This might require doing a little research online.

_____

_____

Now stand back and let momentum take over. Once you take just one step toward your goal, you put a fatal chink in the barrier that's been standing in your way. After you overcome barrier one, go on and make an action plan for barrier two. As you forge ahead, your confidence will grow, and that barrier will crumble to the ground in front of your eyes. Before long, all you'll be able to see are the myriad possibilities that lie ahead of you.

You Can!

There's a 67-year-old woman at my gym who blows me away. She's so beautifully sculpted that some days I want to ask her what she's on. But I see her every day. I know what she's on. She's on an unfailing routine of hard work, consistency, and belief. She's living proof that you don't have to take it easy because you're a certain age. And she's not the only proof I've seen. Study after study confirms that women in their 40s, 50s, 60s, 70s, 80s, and, hell, even 90s can make amazing gains when they put their minds—and their muscles—to it.

The best study I know that illustrates that you can—and most definitely should—challenge yourself right now is one that was done in an assisted living community in Florida. Massachusetts-based researchers put 19 elderly men and women—the average age of whom was 88.5 years—on a strength

Woman Warrior Inspiration

~ *Hathor* ~

The Egyptian mother goddess Hathor is known as the Lady to the Limit (*limit* meaning the edges of the universe). She rules the heavens, giving birth to the sun every misty dawn. Decked out in turquoise and red and wearing a crown of long horns with a sun disk between them, Hathor was one of the most influential deities in ancient Egypt. Known for her indomitable will, nothing stops her once she sets her sights on something. She stands for creativity and rebirth and is the protector of pregnant women and children. She yields fearsome power and has been known to fly into some serious rages. But a little drink, music, dancing, and love soothe her spirits. When you're thinking about your goals and your role in this world as a woman, think of Hathor and shout, "I can!"

training program for 14 weeks. Some of these people were using walkers and in wheelchairs, and they still came in and pushed their muscles to fatigue, doing one set of 8 to 12 reps at a weight heavy enough to make their muscles say, "Uncle." The reward for their efforts? The group lost an average of 3 pounds of body fat and replaced it with 4 pounds of strong, lean muscle. Even better, they became more independently mobile—one was even able to ditch her wheelchair! That's what muscle does for you.

If these people could do it, you can too. And you *need* to. *Right now.* Women naturally lose about half a pound of muscle every year during their adult life. Maybe that sounds like a good thing because you're "losing weight." But it's not. Muscle is what drives your metabolism. Without it, you're going to get weak and flabby and gain fat no matter how you watch your diet, because you just won't burn calories like you used to. Studies show that you can increase your strength 100 percent in just 12 weeks. You'll see results in as little as three to six. What you do right now sets the stage for the rest of your life. So set your goals. Set 'em high. Then turn the pages, and let's go for them! You deserve nothing less.

6

Ain't No Barrier Big Enough

Your Excuses Stop Here

If anyone ever had an excuse not to exercise it was Kirsten Dunst. She was already lean and gorgeous, and she was juggling a grueling schedule that would have worn out the President of the United States. At the time she worked with me intensely, she was filming *Spider-Man 2* and preparing for her role in *Wimbledon*. That meant long hours on the set; working with a tennis coach; training with me; and, oh yeah, trying to have a life and get some sleep somewhere along the way.

But she never made excuses. She always showed up on time and said, "Let's go for it." In the end, she looked better than Anna Kournikova. She was stronger than she'd ever been in her life. She had amazing inner stamina and even more amazing muscle tone in her arms, abs, and legs.

Do you think Kirsten did this because she had special celebrity excuse-banishing powers? No! I see the same process every day with *all* my clients.

Often, at the beginning of the process, excuses come up—"I was too busy at work," "My daughter was sick today," "My mom needed me"—but after working on some true honesty, these excuses melt away. Of course there are days and things come up when you can't work out. But I will show you how to tell a real reason from a made-up excuse that comes from a place devoid of true body love.

At the end of the day, excuses are just your insecurities trying to sabotage your efforts. Don't let them. Whether it's no time, low motivation, past failures, fear of success, or nonsupportive family and friends holding you back, you can break through and keep your spirit on track. Let's investigate what's really behind all those excuses and banish them one by one, once and for all.

The Excuse: I Don't Have Time!

The time excuse is the one I probably hear most frequently and is hands down the biggest death knell to any exercise program. It starts out innocently enough. "Oh, a meeting ran long, and now I have to pick up my daughter from school. I just can't make it today." But before you know it, you're canceling workouts two or three times a week and find yourself sitting on the sofa, feeling completely out of the game, wondering what went wrong.

The truth is that exercise is not yet on your mental "must-do" list, and until it is, you'll simply never find the time to work out consistently. Look, everyone is bone-crushingly busy these days. I work with some of the most time-slammed people in the world. I don't just mean celebrities, who in some cases get paid to get into shape, but business owners, politicians, self-employed people, and high-powered executives who can barely grab three minutes to go to the bathroom. Despite a schedule that's packed fuller than the red-eye to Vegas, they're in the gym on time and without fail. To them, it is a nonnegotiable part of their day, a top priority.

Come clean. Ask yourself, "Did I really have absolutely no time today to squeeze in a 20-minute workout?" Did you watch any TV today? Did you surf the Web even though you weren't really looking for anything? The real deal is that although once in a blue moon something comes up—like an all-day business seminar—where you really, truly can't exercise, most days there's time. The average working woman watches more than 14 hours of TV a week—that's two-plus hours every day. I'm not trying to guilt you out of your favorite shows. I'm just making a point that you already know deep down: we always make time for what we want to do. Do you really want it? If the answer is yes (and if you're reading this book, chances are it is), check out the following strategies.

Break the barrier. It takes 30 days to form a new habit. If you're not used to fitting exercise into your life, it will take at least that long for it to become like brushing your teeth and washing your hair. Make the commitment right now to schedule your workouts for the next month in ink in your dayplanner or in Microsoft Outlook on your desktop instead of waiting until later and "seeing how the day goes." *Later* always becomes *never.* Plan your workout the night before; organize your workout gear in one place; and when the scheduled time comes, do it. Before long, exercise will just be something you do every day without fail—and without excuses.

Note: Sometimes "I don't have time" means "I'm scared to take the time." Too often women worry that they won't get their work done or they'll look selfish if they take 30 minutes or an hour of their day to exercise. Just try it for one month. You'll see what the world's top executives know: taking that time to tend to your body and give your overworked mind a break makes you twice as productive when you get back to the grind.

The Excuse: I'm Tired!

Here's a secret: even exercise professionals get tired and don't feel like working out sometimes. There are plenty of days I'm parked in my cozy apartment thinking, "Damn, I don't want to get changed and go out there and run the park today." But what I know, and what you'll soon learn, is that energy begets energy. I know that five or six footfalls into my run, my energy will surge like I've just taken a trip through Starbucks. And I'll be buzzing with energy longer than any lift from a cappuccino grande.

Come clean. Ask yourself, "Why am I tired?" If you're exhausted because you're a new mom and you were up with a crying baby all night, that's perfectly legitimate. You can do some stretches and call it a day. But if you're "desk-tired"—the kind of blah inertia you get from sitting and working at a computer all day—you don't need to sit more. That'll just make it worse. You need to *move*.

Break the barrier. The secret here is self-talk. Remind yourself that you're tired because you've been sedentary all day. Your heart hasn't been pumping very hard and you've been stewing in everyday stress that saps your spirit, leaving you feeling tapped out even though you really haven't done anything but sit at a computer screen. Tell yourself, "I will just do 10 minutes." Grant yourself permission to call it quits and take a rest day if you are still slogging through your workout after 10 full minutes. But I guarantee that you'll feel so great once you get your engine revving and blood circulating that there'll be no stopping you once you start. Eventually, you'll recognize feeling wiped out as a symptom that you really need to move, not that you should bag your workout.

The Excuse: I'm Too Sore!

Any time you start a new workout or change your routine to make it more challenging, chances are good you're going to be sore the next day or two. It's called *delayed onset muscle soreness* (DOMS), and it's the first step to getting stronger. When you push your muscles to a new level, you create microscopic tears in the fibers, which, along with some related swelling, can leave you stiff and sore. As your body rebuilds, you get stronger (and more toned), and the same workout no longer leaves you aching. Though you should definitely give your muscles a chance to recover when they're sore from a big effort, taking the day off is not the answer.

Come clean. How sore are you? If you can't sit down without hanging on to the chair arms and wincing like you're sucking lemon slices, you should definitely take a day off from strength training, but you should do some light cardio. Your muscles need nutrients to repair and rebuild. The best way to deliver fresh nutrients and carry out the metabolic waste is to increase your circulation. Walking, light cycling, or swimming will pump rich, nutrient-dense blood through your muscles and speed their healing. You'll also feel less sore when you're finished.

Break the barrier. While a little soreness is inevitable, you shouldn't be walking like Pinocchio after every workout. Some simple preventive measures can help minimize the muscle damage and ultimately erase soreness as an excuse:

- **Always warm up and cool down.** Preparing your muscles for the challenge ahead will keep the damage to a minimum when you start pushing it. Cooling down with easy activity and light stretching will ensure that most of the metabolic waste is flushed out of your system.
- **Rub it out.** Ask your honey to give you a light rubdown after a hard workout. The more you can flush your muscles, the less sore they'll be. If you don't have a set of hands at your beck and call, try one of the self-massagers you can get at Bath & Body Works, or treat yourself to a professional massage.
- **Chill.** Professional athletes soak in ice baths after a hard competition to reduce inflammation and speed healing. I don't expect you to go that far, but if you really turned it on today, putting some ice packs (packages of frozen peas will do) on those thighs and knees can help you feel better tomorrow.
- **Pop some C.** Studies suggest that vitamin C may help decrease soreness by minimizing damage and speeding repair. Take 500 milligrams (you can keep a bottle of chewable Cs right in your gym bag) after every workout.

The Excuse: My Husband/ Partner/Kids Give Me a Hard Time When I Go Work Out

Sometimes the people closest to you are the ones who sabotage you most, and sometimes that someone is you. What am I trying to say? That sometimes your family will actually resent you working out (especially if they're not and they feel guilty about it), so they'll subtly (or not so subtly) undermine your efforts. But sometimes you're reading too much into what they say or do because you feel guilty spending time on yourself instead of them. And sometimes conflict arises from a combination of your actions and their reactions. Any way you shake it, this is one that can be conquered with good communication.

Come clean. Look closely at and honestly assess your husband's/partner's/ kids' reactions. Women have a huge guilt complex whenever they take time for themselves. So first make certain that there actually is an issue before you start trying to resolve it. If they're just harassing you or whining a little because they have to heat up their own dinner, move on without giving it a second thought. If they are genuinely upset, you won't feel better until you figure out why. One explanation is they feel threatened. When one family member goes off and tries to improve herself or himself by exercising and eating right, the others often feel bad about themselves, especially if they're chowing down cheeseburgers and fries in front of the tube. Your husband and kids may not like feeling like they have to change their ways, so they're trying to stop you. One client's husband does this routinely because he feels bad about himself, and as we all know, misery loves company. If this is your situation, you need to have a heartfelt, reassuring conversation with your loved ones (see the tips that follow). Finally, there may be another, less insidious reason for your family's upset: they don't know your workout schedule. They may be planning for you to be available at a certain time like you always are, and suddenly you're not, so they feel forgotten.

Break the barrier. Communication is your best weapon in this battle. When your family understands where you're coming from, they'll be far more likely to support and less likely to sabotage your efforts. Here are some tips on what to say:

∞ **Keep it about you.** Have a sit-down conversation with your family. Explain to them that you're starting this Show It Love program because you want to feel better about yourself and be the healthiest, happiest mom and wife you can be. Reassure them that you're not trying to change anyone and this isn't some grand judgment.

- **Share it.** No one likes feeling left out. If your family doesn't know what you're doing, they may feel like you're keeping something from them. Tell them about the exercises you're doing. Show them a few moves. They may be intrigued and inspired to join you. Either way, when you share your experiences, your family will feel included and less left out.

- **Let them know what to expect.** No one likes surprises—like their honey tossing all the nacho chips from the pantry and replacing them with edamame. If you're going to change what's in the kitchen, tell your family, and give them the option to have their own food stashed somewhere you won't see it or be tempted by it. Also, give them your workout schedule. That way they can work around your program.

- **Be unwavering.** I'll be honest. Even with all this open and fair communication, your family may be a little put off by all the change and put pressure on you to pull the plug. Don't do it! Stay the course. You have to know your own journey and go it alone, if need be. But it will strengthen you, and before long, your family will accept the "new you" and the changes will become routine to them, so they'll stop hassling you. Who knows? As they witness your transformation, they may be inspired to take a few steps toward their own self-realization.

The Excuse: I've Been Through Enough—I Deserve a Break!

I have a client who is coming back from a grueling battle with breast cancer. She's not yet 40, and she's angry: angry that this happened to her, angry that she has to worry about fertility issues and rebuilding her body at an age when she should be hitting her prime. I understand her anger. I understand when people who have been through disease, divorce, and natural disasters come in and say, "Damn it, I need a break. I've had enough!" But the answer isn't quitting on your body. Exercise, movement, eating right—those things are not punishment. They are nourishment to help you get through the hard times. Believe me, I know. I've been through disease, divorce, and disaster, and each time I get stronger and march on. We can all make excuses, but there comes a time when you have to stop writing yourself off with excuses from yesterday and take charge of yourself right now.

Come clean. When you feel like throwing in the towel because you've "had enough," ask yourself what you hope to accomplish. What's plan B for making yourself feel better? If you're not going to work out because you need a break, what will you do? If the answer is "Take a nice vacation to Tahiti and stare at the ocean for seven days," I say, "Go!" Really. That tells me you're serious about doing something positive to help yourself heal. By all means, do it. If the answer is "I don't know" or "Nothing"—or worse, you're just going to veg in front of the TV—that's not acceptable. Your body deserves more. *You* deserve more.

Break the barrier. When you have a setback, whether it's a surgery or weight gain because of a breakup, resist the urge to lament, "Why me?" and instead say, "What now? What am I going to do to heal, move on, and be better?" The answer starts with movement, forward momentum fueled by life-giving oxygen. When you exercise, you create energy, you infuse every cell with the fresh air and nutrients it needs to live. Don't disrespect your body in its time of need by shutting down and cutting off its life force! Even if you can't work out on the physical level, do your emotional exercises. Breathe deeply and talk to yourself. Build yourself up. Then move as much as you can as you're able. Before you know it, you'll be right back in the game.

The fact of the matter is that fitness is a little bit like religion. Having it doesn't guarantee that bad things won't happen to you, but it does guarantee that you'll get up on your feet faster and stronger after something unexpected knocks you down.

A Workout for All Reasons

Now that I've taken away all your excuses for not working out, I'm going to give you a pass to change your workout to match your mental and emotional needs. At the end of this book, you'll find Your Daily Get-Through-Anything Guide. In it, you'll find specific advice and a guide to particular exercises in the book that will help see you through your most miserable days, whether you just got dumped or you're suffering a serious case of baby-weight blues.

7

Soul Food

Feeding Your Spirit Right

Let's get something straight. There is no such thing as forbidden food. I am no vegan. I am no health freak. I don't follow any special secret diet. I eat steak and bread, and I enjoy a good cocktail now and then. I've also found that women who obsessively follow stringent diets inevitably look worse than they did before they started—whether or not they succeed in losing all the weight they want. They just look grim and pinched. Completely joyless. How sexy is that? The bottom line is you need to indulge your taste buds and enjoy wonderful food, while also exercising a little moderation.

I think the real secret is trying to make every morsel you put in your mouth special. And that doesn't mean you have to shell out a ton of money for fancy food. It's a philosophy that applies to absolutely everything you eat. Even if it's just some crackers out of a box, arrange them on a plate, add some tomato slices, a little basil, some fresh mozzarella, and make it something that satisfies your soul. Something that sends the message, "I'm special. I deserve to nourish my body. I deserve to reach my goals." That is what I Can eating is all about. Here are some of my golden food rules for feeding your soul.

Eat Outside the Box

I want you to make me a promise right now. Raise your right hand and pledge this minute that you will never eat straight out of another container. Seriously, no more standing in front of the fridge with the Tupperware container half-open, grabbing fingerfuls of leftover chicken. No more scooping food directly from the Chinese take-out carton into your mouth. And absolutely no more sitting in front of the TV with the giant bag of chips mindlessly munching away.

This alone will help you feel more in control of your eating habits, not to mention lose unwanted weight fast if you're a chronic "container eater." Studies show that people eat about 30 percent more—that's 200 calories (or more) for a full meal, enough to put on 20 pounds a year—when they don't have a good gauge of how much they're eating, which is why eating right out of containers is so dangerous. Have you ever polished off a tiny pint of lo mien noodles without a second thought? Next time dish out the contents of that little pint onto your plate. Your jaw will hit the floor when you see how many noodles they pack into that puny cardboard box! The same goes for cookies and snack foods. You would never, ever sit down and scarf down 20 Oreos if they were stacked up on a plate. But I've known women to chow down a whole sleeve of them while standing in front of the pantry and eating straight from the box. We are designed by nature to be able to pack away all the food presented to us. Do yourself a favor and present yourself the proper amount on a plate from now on.

Most important, putting food on a plate also puts the focus back on the food instead of just filling a void, whether it's true hunger or boredom. Eating should be a sensory experience, and it should be about the food. How does it look? How does it taste? How does it make you feel? When's the last time you even thought about food in those terms? We don't do it too often in this country, and that's a big reason why many of us are too heavy and why our shelves are lined with junk food that doesn't even taste all that good instead of fresh, beautiful food that fulfills us.

On a related note, try not to eat in front of the television. Anything that distracts you from your meal removes you from the sensory experience of the food and exponentially increases the likelihood that you will overeat. It's also not good for your spirit. Take 15 or 20 minutes, sit down in peace, and really enjoy your food.

Clean Your Plate

This isn't about finishing all your food for the starving children. This is about starting to think about eating clean. Now that you're exercising more and honoring your body, it will start craving food that replenishes all the nutrients you're using to burn fat and build lean muscle tissue. It'll start wanting real food that fills you up with more than refined, artificially flavored calories. Now is the time, as you transition from the emotional eating of I Am to the power eating of I Do, to make meaningful changes in your eating habits that will help your mind, body, and spirit be as strong and healthy as they can be. Here are some simple steps to make that happen.

Ditch the Fake Stuff

Again, I'm not one to say you should never eat this or never eat that. But some foods are so unhealthy that you're better off tossing them in the trash and keeping them out of your kitchen. Number one on that list: soda. It's nothing but sugar and chemicals. Others I'd make a clean sweep of—packaged cakes and cookies. I'm not saying never eat sweets. I'm saying, if you want these things, occasionally (like once or twice a month) go to the bakery and buy a few freshly made cookies or pastries. You'll eat fewer of these foods and they'll be made with real ingredients like sugar and butter instead of partially hydrogenated fat (trans fat) and high-fructose corn syrup (HFCS).

Speaking of HFCS, read your labels and avoid it whenever possible (it's in damn near everything from bread to ketchup, so I know you probably can't eliminate it entirely). High-fructose corn syrup is a supercheap sweetener that was dumped into our food supply about 30 years ago so that big food manufacturers could pinch pennies, and it's no coincidence that that's the same time the obesity level started to rise. Unlike real, plain sugar—which causes an insulin response that triggers a biological message from your brain that you're full and should stop eating—manmade HFCS gets into cells without triggering an insulin response. That means you eat . . . and eat . . . and eat without ever getting the signal that you're full. Making matters worse (oh yeah, it gets worse), HFCS bypasses your body's normal energy-burning response and is more readily turned into fat. Research shows the average American eats more than *60 pounds* of this toxic stuff a year. I say, don't be average! Keep it off your plate as much as possible.

Eat from the Earth

Once you clear the junk from your diet, you'll have room for the good stuff. As I mentioned in the I Am section of this book, I'm a big believer in eating foods that look like they came from the earth—foods like fruits and vegetables and grains, fish and meats that you can look at and immediately tell where they came from. Likewise, your plate should resemble a garden, filled with plant-based foods and bright, rich colors. Why? Because the pigments that give those fruits and vegetables and herbs and spices their gorgeous colors are actually potent antioxidants that heal your working muscles and keep you healthy.

In a report from the University of Oslo, which tested more than 1,000 common foods and beverages for their antioxidant potency, every single one of the top 10 foods comes from a plant. Check out this list, including the serving size needed to get a healthy dose, and stock up your pantry. Aim to eat one or two of these foods every day (when you get to number 6, you'll see how easy it is to get at least one).

1 Blackberries (1 cup)
2 Walnuts (1 ounce, or about 18 halves)
3 Strawberries (1 cup, sliced)
4 Artichoke hearts (1 cup)
5 Cranberries (1 cup)
6 Brewed coffee (1 cup)
7 Raspberries (1 cup)
8 Pecans (1 ounce, or about 20)
9 Blueberries (1 cup)
10 Ground cloves (1 teaspoon)

Fruits and vegetables are also the prime source of the essential vitamins your body needs just to survive, let alone maintain a healthy body weight. And as much as we Americans eat, we simply aren't getting enough of them. A recent study from Arizona State University at Mesa found that people with the highest levels of vitamin C in their blood had the lowest body fat percentages; unfortunately, about 30 percent of Americans don't even get the daily recommended amount of vitamin C—one of the easiest vitamins to get, since it's found in citrus fruits and orange juice.

So no more messing around. If you want to meet your weight-loss goals, make it a rule to eat at least one color at every breakfast, lunch, dinner, and snack. I don't care if it's a handful of baby carrots or a sliced kiwi, throw it in there. And keep an eye out for every opportunity to swap some bland, refined fare for fresh food. Get a side of veggies instead of fries or chips with your sandwich. Ask for extra lettuce and tomato instead of cheese on your sub. Be creative and always think color.

Eating from the earth also guarantees you'll get enough fiber. Experts recommend 25 to 30 grams a day; most Americans are lucky to get half that amount. Fiber does more than "keep you regular." It also controls blood sugar levels, which is absolutely essential for having high energy and a good mood for your workouts and everyday life. Fiber also fills you up, so you're a whole lot less likely to overeat. What does 25 grams look like? One cup of oatmeal, half a cup of raspberries, an ounce of almonds, two slices of whole-grain bread, and one pear. Try counting your fiber grams just for a day or two, and see how much better you feel.

Spice It Right

One of the biggest complaints I hear is that healthy eating is "boring." Well, I promise you that there's nothing boring or bland about the way I or any of my clients eat. Our food is out of this world with flavor, and we wouldn't have it any other way. The secret is spice. You need to get brave with your food. You need to head to the spice shelves at the store and fill up your rack. You'll find a list of my favorites on page 34. But don't limit yourself. The labels on most spices will provide examples of foods to try them with. Don't be afraid to season with abandon. If you're still "spicephobic," start with scrambled eggs. They're the perfect blank canvas for experimenting with new flavors and discovering what works best to your taste. Remember, fancy restaurants don't usually serve different foods than you do; they have potatoes and asparagus and chicken. It's the flavors they use that make their meals special. Going back to the philosophy of I Can, you should make every meal that you cook for yourself special too. The right spices do the trick.

Drink Up

Everyone's heard we should drink eight glasses of water a day. That amount includes the water you get from food and other drinks like coffee and even soda (but not alcohol). Most experts say that five to six of those glasses should ideally be in the form of plain, fresh water. I say if you're working up a sweat every day, you need even more. I recommend buying a 24- to 32-ounce Nalgene water bottle, filling it up, and finishing it twice a day. The human body is 65 percent water, and staying hydrated is one of the most basic ways to keep it looking and performing its best. On the flip side, dehydration leads to headaches, fatigue, poor skin and muscle tone, and constipation. Just think of how you feel the morning after a late night and you have the idea. There's nothing sexy or spirit-lifting about that.

Water is also one of the most overlooked weight-loss aids. It not only staves off false hunger pangs (many of us mistake thirst for hunger), it actually helps your body metabolize stored fat. When you're dehydrated, your kidneys struggle to filter all the waste from your body, so they turn to the liver for help. The liver's job is to help turn stored fat into energy. Well, I have news for you. If your liver's busy helping the kidneys get rid of your waste, you're going to end up with less fat loss. Research shows that your fat deposits actually increase when you decrease your water intake, and they shrink when you drink more. You also won't burn as many calories without enough water. Sports performance studies show that being just 2 to 4 percent dehydrated can reduce your strength training power by more than 20 percent and cut your aerobic energy in half. Good hydration also helps keep your blood volume high so you can wash the metabolic waste out of your system after a hard workout. This means you're less apt to be stiff and achy, and you'll feel more like hitting it again the next day.

These days there's simply no excuse not to flush your system with the two quarts of liquid your hardworking body needs each day. Every street vendor, gas station, minimart, convenience store, and soda machine is stocked with bottled water. If you don't like it plain, you can buy sparkling water, carbonated water, or flavored water—or just add a squeeze of lemon to brighten up the taste. It's cheap, calorie-free, and one of the easiest ways to stay healthy and drop unwanted pounds. Drink up!

Eat In

I live in the world capital of takeout. Here in New York City, you can get any type of food you can imagine, to go, at any time of the day. And I know that trend is spreading outside of urban borders to the point where you can drive up to your favorite chain restaurant and grab a full meal to go. The convenience is great, but it comes at a price, and that's calories. When you pick up restaurant food, you have no idea how much butter, salt, lard, and Lord knows what else is in there. The simplest soup could pack half a day's worth of sodium. I tell my clients, "Don't get married to takeout." Just stock your shelves and keep your meals simple, and you'll be able to make a dinner every night that takes no more time and effort than rifling through your stack of take-out menus, making the call, fishing out your cash, and sitting around waiting for your food to come. Ultimately, it'll be a lot better for you too.

One of the easiest ways to cook up a fast meal? Stir-fry. All you need is a hot skillet and a tablespoon of oil. Sliced meat, fish, and veggies are literally cooked in a flash. Add a dash of soy sauce and a pinch of pepper; pour it over brown rice or whole wheat fettuccine, and you've got a quick, satisfying, colorful dish. Check out the recipes in Chapter 2 and at the end of this chapter for more fast meal ideas.

With just a little advance preparation, you can also save yourself cooking time during the week. Make a big crock of soup like my favorite vegetable and brown lentil (page 127) on Sunday afternoon and freeze it in single-serving Tupperware containers, so you can just nuke it anytime during the week. Add a piece of fruit and a slice of whole-grain bread, and you have a complete, healthy meal.

It takes very little time to feed your body right, and you're worth it. Here are some of my favorite recipes.

Kacy's Vegetable and Brown Lentil Soup

This hearty soup is a meal in itself and won't compromise your waistline at all. It is low in fat and high in vitamins.

2 tablespoons extra-virgin olive oil

2 cloves garlic

1 large onion, diced

1 stalk celery, diced

2 14.5-ounce cans vegetable broth

1 28-ounce can crushed tomatoes

½ cup frozen green beans

1 bay leaf

1 cube vegetable bouillon

¼ cup fresh parsley

1 large carrot, diced

Black pepper to taste

1 cup brown lentils

1 14.5-ounce can dark kidney beans

3 small zucchini, cubed

Heat olive oil in a large saucepan or pot, then add garlic, onion, and celery, and sauté for about 1 minute. Add the rest of the ingredients, except for the lentils, kidney beans, and zucchini. Bring to a boil.

Reduce heat, cover, and simmer 15 to 20 minutes. Add lentils, kidney beans, and zucchini. Bring back to a boil, then reduce heat, cover, and simmer again for 15 to 20 minutes. Be sure to remove the bay leaf before eating.

Makes 9 servings (serving size = 1½ cups)

NUTRITION FACTS PER SERVING: **CALORIES** 155 (22% from fat); **FAT** 3.8 g (saturated, 0.5 g; polyunsaturated, 0.4 g; monounsaturated, 2.4 g); **PROTEIN** 7.1 g; **CARBOHYDRATES** 24 g; **FIBER** 7.6 g; **CHOLESTEROL** 0 mg; **IRON** 2.4 mg; **SODIUM** 317 mg; **CALCIUM** 90 mg

New York–Minute Tuna Salad

This colorful salad incorporates canned tuna as well as fresh veggies and is a light, quick, and delicious way to satisfy your midday hunger cravings.

1 5-ounce bag prewashed mixed greens of your choice

1½ bell peppers, thinly sliced (I use a combination of red, orange, and yellow peppers.)

¼ cup fresh flat leaf or American parsley

2 small or 1 medium-sized tomato, sliced

1 small red onion or 2 scallions, sliced (optional)

2 6-ounce cans tuna in olive oil

Salt and pepper to taste

1 lemon wedge

Combine all vegetables in a large bowl and top with tuna. Mix and season with salt and pepper. Finish with a squeeze of lemon.

Makes 2 servings

NUTRITION FACTS PER SERVING: **CALORIES** 296 (15.4% from fat); **FAT** 5 g (saturated, 0.1 g; polyunsaturated, 0.3 g; monounsaturated, 0.1 g); **PROTEIN** 53.8 g; **CARBOHYDRATES** 12.3 g; **FIBER** 4 g; **CHOLESTEROL** 60 mg; **IRON** 2 mg; **SODIUM** 863 mg; **CALCIUM** 72 mg

Sautéed Shrimp with Asparagus and Brown Rice

1 tablespoon light olive oil

½ cup sliced asparagus

1 small tomato, diced

Salt and pepper to taste

5 to 6 fresh large shrimp, cleaned and deveined

Cayenne pepper (optional)

1 to 2 scallions, sliced

½ cup cooked brown rice

Heat olive oil in a medium sauté pan. Sauté asparagus 4 to 5 minutes over medium heat. Add diced tomato and season with salt and pepper; cook another 3 minutes. Season shrimp with salt, pepper, and cayenne pepper (if desired). Add shrimp to pan and reduce heat to medium-low; cook 5 minutes. Top with sliced scallions and serve over brown rice.

Makes 1 serving

NUTRITION FACTS PER SERVING: **CALORIES** 320 (43% from fat); **FAT** 16 g (saturated, 2.4 g; polyunsaturated, 2.8 g; monounsaturated, 10.5 g); **PROTEIN** 14 g; **CARBOHYDRATES** 33.3 g; **FIBER** 5.6 g; **CHOLESTEROL** 64 mg; **IRON** 4 mg; **SODIUM** 368 mg; **CALCIUM** 94 mg

Quick Marinated Chicken

Use this easy marinade with fresh chicken for a delicious dish that is full of flavor.

5 tablespoons extra-virgin olive oil

2 tablespoons red wine vinegar

¼ cup fresh cilantro, chopped fine

½ teaspoon salt

½ teaspoon pepper

½ teaspoon garlic powder

1 skinless, boneless chicken breast

In a small bowl, combine all the ingredients except the chicken and mix well. Coat and cover chicken with marinade, and refrigerate at least 20 minutes. Sauté, broil, or grill chicken, and serve with the vegetable of your choice.

Makes 1 serving

NUTRITION FACTS PER SERVING: **CALORIES** 317 (46% from fat); **FAT** 16 g (saturated, 2.5 g; polyunsaturated, 1.7 g; monounsaturated, 11.3 g); **PROTEIN** 39.5 g; **CARBOHYDRATES** 1 g; **FIBER** 0.2 g; **CHOLESTEROL** 99 mg; **IRON** 1.4 mg; **SODIUM** 402 mg; **CALCIUM** 22 mg

Grilled Lamb Chops with Rosemary and Lemon

When I'm craving a meat-based meal, I turn to savory lamb chops to satisfy me without weighing me down.

4 single-cut lamb chops

Salt and pepper to taste

1 tablespoon extra-virgin olive oil

½ teaspoon rosemary, dried or fresh

1 lemon wedge

In a large bowl or platter, season lamb chops with salt and pepper, olive oil, and rosemary.

On a stovetop grill or in a sauté pan over medium heat, cook about 4 to 5 minutes per side, or until desired doneness. Top lamb with pan juices, and garnish with lemon wedge.

Makes 4 servings

NUTRITION FACTS PER SERVING: **CALORIES** 502 (53% from fat); **FAT** 30 g (saturated, 7.6 g; polyunsaturated, 2.7 g; monounsaturated, 17 g); **PROTEIN** 54.4 g; **CARBOHYDRATES** 1.2 g; **FIBER** 0.5 g; **CHOLESTEROL** 172 mg; **IRON** 5 mg; **SODIUM** 468 mg; **CALCIUM** 42 mg

Baby Arugula and White Kidney Bean Salad

This is a quick, hearty salad that is filled with protein and essential vitamins.

3 tablespoons extra-virgin olive oil

1 12-ounce can white kidney beans

½ teaspoon rosemary, dried or fresh

Salt and pepper to taste

1 5-ounce bag prewashed baby arugula

1 small red onion, thinly sliced

1 tablespoon red wine vinegar

Heat 1 tablespoon olive oil in a small saucepan. Add kidney beans and rosemary; season with salt and pepper. Cook over low heat 10 minutes, or until beans are tender but not mushy.

In a medium bowl, combine arugula and onion. Add the cooked beans, remaining oil, and vinegar; mix well.

Makes 2 servings

NUTRITION FACTS PER SERVING: **CALORIES** 386 (54% from fat); **FAT** 23 g (saturated, 3 g; polyunsaturated, 2.1 g; monounsaturated, 16.2 g); **PROTEIN** 12 g; **CARBOHYDRATES** 34.2 g; **FIBER** 10 g; **CHOLESTEROL** 0 mg; **IRON** 4 mg; **SODIUM** 231 mg; **CALCIUM** 189 mg

8

Woman Warrior Series 2

Tap into Your True Potential

When I first started working with Julianne Moore, she had just had her second baby. Here was a real, centered, grounded woman. She loved being a mom. She allowed herself the very perfect "flaws" that come with being a woman—that is, putting on weight as you create and nurture life. She wasn't all stressed out about pregnancy and motherhood. She embraced every moment. At the same time, she wasn't living in a fantasyland. She realized she would have to get her body back because she would eventually need to go back to work.

As emotionally grounded as she was, Julianne still hadn't quite accepted how much physical ability she had locked inside. She hadn't yet tapped into her true I Can spirit, because she believed reaching her physical goals just wasn't in her cards. Case in point: She had always wanted strong, chiseled arms, but she'd been unsuccessful in the past. So she started blaming her genes. "I'm a freckly, redheaded Irish woman," she'd say. "My body won't do that. I'm not made to have that kind of muscle tone."

I said, "Oh, ye of little faith. Half the work is done. You're here. You've been honest with yourself. You realize what you want. Let's go get it done."

After a few weeks of the Power Presses and Open with Strength upper-body work detailed in the routine you're soon to learn, she came in simply raving: "Oh, my God! Look at these arms!" Now, this woman who embraces life more than anyone I know has strong, beautiful arms so she can squeeze it even harder. She also became completely in tune with her inner power. At 42, after giving birth to her daughter, Julianne had only a few short months before embarking on a whirlwind media tour to promote her amazing high-profile films *The Hours* and *Far from Heaven*. She needed to get back in shape—fast. But now that she realized all the power she held within, it was no sweat. Barely three months later, she was sporting a lean, sinewy body. She knew she had the potential. She worked hard and made it happen.

The Next Level

I Can is about preparing your spirit to lay down a body that can take on whatever life throws its way and conquer challenges you never thought possible. Remember the mind-body connection we established in I Am? Remember that "aha" moment when you came to realize how what you thought about your body and how you talked to your body physically affected how it performed and ultimately how it looked? Well, guess what? It doesn't stop there. You also have a spirit-body connection that is equally strong and just as important to reaching your ultimate goals.

On some level, we all know that a strong body can bolster an embattled spirit. I can tell by the endless stream of clients who walk through my door in times of trouble so I can help them find their footing again. I'm a personal trainer. Technically people should come to me to lose weight and shape their thighs. But many come in to have their spirits strengthened. Back in

1998, the media were jumping all over the fact that I'd been spotted training Monica Lewinsky in Central Park. No matter what you think of her or what happened, here was a 25-year-old woman embroiled in a scandal that rocked the presidency of the United States. She was the subject of so much scorn and ridicule—so much of it because she wasn't some stereotypically skinny beauty queen (somehow it seems as though, in many people's eyes, the whole thing would have been okay or at least more acceptable if she had been)—it's amazing that she didn't just hole up in her apartment and never come out. But she did come out, and she knocked on my door. She came to me not to transform her body (though she was putting on some unwanted weight under the stress) but to toughen up her spirit for the long, hard road ahead. She wanted to be able to say and believe, "I can face whatever lies ahead and rise above my mistakes and go forward with my life." And in the spirit of believing that all women can and should continue to learn and grow and boldly move on, I helped her.

I can help you too. Here's the real deal. When you feel physically weak, your spirit suffers. And though you may not feel weak right now, you never know what lies around the corner in this life or what challenges await. If nothing else, you need to get as physically and spiritually strong as you can right now so you aren't left feeling weak in the future when you need to be strong.

Few women realize the toll that time can take on your strength. Worse, too many women accept it as a "fact of life" that they'll get weaker over time and not be able to do all the things they do now. That is BS! Yes, we all lose a step or two as we age, but the dramatic decline so many of us think is inevitable is a result of not taking control of our own strength right now and staying in the game. I saw some statistics a few weeks ago that will blow you away. More than 40 percent of women ages 55 to 74 and 65 percent of women ages 75 to 84 were unable to lift *10 pounds* in a study of more than 5,000 men and women in Framingham, Massachusetts. That means they can't even lift a bag of groceries—or a baby. It gets more frightening. Other research shows that after age 60, 68 percent of women can't open a tight-lidded jar of pasta sauce without help. Leg strength declines so much in sedentary women that just getting up out of a chair is tough for many by age 50 and downright impossible by 80.

What does it do to your spirit when it's an effort to stand up, open jars, and carry a bag of cat food? I'm not trying to scare you (though these statistics *are* scary); I'm trying to educate and empower you. The facts are the facts. Strength naturally peaks in women at about age 25. It plateaus through 35 or 40, and then it begins an accelerating decline, with most women losing between 25 to 30 percent of their peak strength by 60 or 65, mostly due to disuse and lost muscle tissue. You have the power to throw the brakes on your sliding strength by building all the beautiful, strong lean muscle you can right now and maintaining it throughout your life. Studies show that active men who do strength training perform better in exercise tests than normally active (but non–strength training) men half their age. I haven't seen similar studies on women, but I can tell you from experience that it's true for us as well. And it is absolutely, positively never too late to start and to regain lost strength and the I Can spirit.

Through these I Can exercises (which, as you'd expect, are more challenging and demanding than those in I Am), you are building strength for your future. But more important, you're building strength for right now—your present daily life. I want you to get stronger no matter how in shape or out of shape you feel at the moment. You don't know how powerful you're capable of feeling until you start pushing yourself. I can't count the number of clients who have said to me, "Wow! And I thought I was in shape!" when after a few weeks of performing my signature moves they see how much fitter and stronger they are.

To Gym or Not to Gym

This entire Show It Love program can be done in your living room. It's that way by design. But it can also be done in a gym, and now that you're growing more spiritually and physically empowered, a gym membership is something you might want to consider.

For one, you'll be surrounded by kindred spirits—that is, other women (and men) who are trying to make themselves stronger for the game of life just like you. Being around others on the move can inspire you to move even more. In fact, a recent Stanford University study of nearly 3,000 women found that women (who are social by nature) are more motivated to exercise when they see others doing the same. You'll also be able to share your favorite exercises with others. The moves and routines in Show It Love are so unique that my clients often attract "interested bystanders" when they're working out in the club. That makes some of my clients crazy, because they "paid" for all that new exercise instruction and they don't want someone getting it for nothing. But I say, "If you care, you stare!" And anyway, I actually encourage my clients to share what I teach them. That's right, give away some of that know-how. It's a blessing to be able to pass along the exercises that are doing wonders for you. As you teach them to someone else, you get better at them yourself. You lose nothing and gain all the good karma and benefits of being a teacher.

Most important, joining a gym can help keep things fresh. A good club offers a wide variety of cardio and strength machines, group exercise classes, mats, bands, balls, and other general fitness equipment and accommodations. That kind of variety is designed to keep the clientele excited and motivated to keep coming back and getting results. When shopping for a club, *be emotional.* So often, especially as women, we try to "think like a man" when we make financial decisions, like buying a health club membership. We want to use our head and think logically, which is fine to a point, but if you're going to join a gym, I want you to join with your heart, not just your mind.

Just as I want Show It Love to do more than flatten your abs, a good gym experience should do more than make you sweat. It should leave you feeling radiant and alive. You shouldn't feel broken down or beat up, but energized, balanced, and ready to take on the day ahead. Here's what to consider before signing on the dotted line:

- **First impression.** I'm a big believer in the power of first impressions. If you walk into a place and think, "Wow, yes," chances are good you've found a club that will be a good fit for you. If you think, "I don't belong here," you probably don't. So pay attention to how you feel when you first walk through that door. Do you like the music? Does the layout make you comfortable? Are you immediately at ease in the gym community? This is a place you're (hopefully) going to be spending a lot of time in over the years. You should love it.

- **Staff.** Do you feel as though you've just walked into a used car dealership or a health club? The staff who attend to you should be sharp, friendly, knowledge-able, and confident. They shouldn't be pushy or, often worse, blasé. The train-ers you meet should be credentialed and experienced. Of course, everyone there wants you to buy a membership; it's their job. But they shouldn't hard-sell you. You should like what you see enough that the place sells itself.

- **Services.** Any added services that would make you more likely to go to the gym or make your gym experience more enjoyable are worth considering. Do you have young children? Many clubs offer child-care services. What kind of personal training is available? The club's services should help you meet your goals and enjoy your time there.

- **Convenience.** Even if you find the Taj Mahal of health clubs, you won't go if it isn't convenient. Trust me! Your commitment to the club is like any new rela-tionship. The first few weeks, you'll be excited enough to make a special trip to get there. But then in a month or two, you'll be like, "What club? I'm not driv-ing 20 minutes out of my way to go to the club." It must be close to your home, close to your work, or en route to somewhere you go frequently. It goes without saying that it should also be open during hours when you can easily make it.

- **Crowds.** The same gym that is pleasantly populated at 10:00 A.M. may be a madhouse at 5:30 P.M. If you plan to use the club during peak hours (7:00 to 9:00 A.M. and 4:00 to 7:00 P.M.), make absolutely sure you visit during those times to be certain you can even get near the treadmills. Don't get me wrong.

There are people who love a mobbed facility and thrive off all the energy, and that's fine. Just be sure you'll be able to get a good workout in when you want it.

∞ **Cost.** I've intentionally listed this one last. Too many people put price at the top of their list when shopping for a club. Although I understand that you have a budget and cost is a very important consideration, it shouldn't necessarily be the ultimate deciding factor. If you join a gym you don't love because you can save $50 a month, but you don't go very often because it doesn't inspire you, have you actually saved money? Or are you really losing cash? I say it's the latter, because you're not getting your money's worth. If you love it and you'll go because you like being there, it's worth a few extra bucks by far. Remember, your body is a precious investment. Your health and strength are priceless. We shell out so much money on things that make us prettier on the outside—new shoes, bags, the latest jeans, skin care, makeup—a good health club experience will make you prettier from the inside out.

Finally, just as you wouldn't buy a car without first taking it around the block, do not sign up for a health club membership without taking it for a "test-drive." Any club worth its salt will give you a trial membership so you can come and use the facilities for a few days before deciding that, yes, it's the place for you.

The I Can Woman Warrior Moves: Let the Spirit Move You

"I love it, Kacy! I want more!" That's literally what some of my clients say as they're mastering their Woman Warrior exercises, and that is how these I Can moves are designed to make you feel. You laid down your strong emotional foundation in I Am. Now we're going to build some spiritual empowerment on top of that with another level of challenging strength moves.

Expect to be a little sore again for the first few days. You're challenging your muscles in new ways, trying to tone and target every last fiber. It's going to hurt a little bit (in a good way) until they build up to the new challenge. You can ease that postexercise ache by being sure to stretch after every workout session and staying on top of your nutritional needs with plenty of water, fresh fruits and vegetables, protein, healthy fats, and whole-grain carbs. Check out the recipes in Chapter 7 for some simple, nutritious recipes that will keep your growing muscles healthy.

Unless otherwise specified, every move starts in the power position. Stand tall and keep your knees soft. Pull your navel to your spine to activate your abs and maintain a straight back and tight, firm belly throughout the moves. If you find that you cannot maintain proper form, do fewer reps and build up to the recommended amount. I would rather have you do 8 or 9 reps with perfect, powerful form than 12 with an arched back or collapsed core. Once again, the I Can Woman Warrior series begins with a trio of core exercises that are designed to warm the body and create a buzz in your emotional, spiritual, and creative power center. You should feel your strength rising from the inside out.

The Details

Reps. Perform 12 reps of each move. For single leg moves, perform 12 reps per side for a total of 24. I am a proponent of pumping and elongating muscles, not with heavy weights but through a full range of motion and high number of repetitions. So don't go crazy with the weights. They should be light to moderate so you can maintain fluid, sweeping motion and good form.

Sets. Try to do three sets of each move. If you can only do two, try lowering the weight. If you still find your form falling apart after two sets, that's fine. Stick to two sets until you feel strong enough to tack on a third. It's not a race. You will get there when your body is ready.

The weight. The weight you choose should be heavy enough so the final three reps of a set feel very challenging. As you get stronger, the moves will feel easier. When those last reps feel like a walk in the park, it's time to pick up heavier weights. Remember, most women are much stronger than they give themselves credit for. Don't be afraid to tap into that strength and say, "I can!"

Progression. For the first week, perform the routine in traditional strength training fashion, completing all three sets of each exercise before moving on to the next one. Starting with week two, perform the moves as a circuit, completing one set of each move, then immediately moving to the next exercise, completing the entire sequence a total of three times. Every time you increase your weights, go back to traditional, three-sets-in-a-row lifting for one week before again performing the routine as a circuit.

Times per week. You will be performing the Woman Warrior exercises three days a week, along with I Can cardio exercises three days a week. See the I Can Workout Log on page 184 for your complete I Can exercise program.

Movement prep. Before starting, do five minutes of light cardio exercise, like jumping rope, light calisthenics, or running in place, to warm up your muscles and get them ready for action.

Lie on your back with your arms extended over your head, palms facing each other. Bend your knees and place your feet flat on the floor, slightly apart.

THE MOVE: Creative Curl

YOU'LL FEEL IT: Down the entire length of the front of your torso. This move is designed to fire every fiber in your abdominal region to really sculpt and whittle your middle.

THE BODY-LOVE BENEFIT: How many times have you heard that you should "listen to your gut"? Well, your gut, or your creative spiritual center, is what you're strengthening right here. Firming it will help firm your resolve too.

Pull your navel toward your spine, contract your abs, and lift your shoulders off the floor, pulling your elbows down to your sides as you do.

continued »

KACY'S COACHING TIPS: Keep your movements strong and controlled. Add intensity by holding a 5- to 8-pound dumbbell with both hands.

Maintaining the curl, reach out with both arms, and then pull your elbows back to your sides.

Return to the starting position.

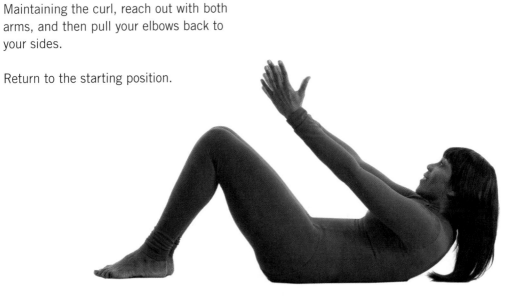

THE MOVE: Creative Curl, *continued*

144

Lie facedown on the floor with your upper body propped on your forearms so your elbows are positioned directly beneath your shoulders. Lift your entire body up off the floor so it forms a straight line from your head to your heels, supported by your forearms and toes. Your back should not arch or droop.

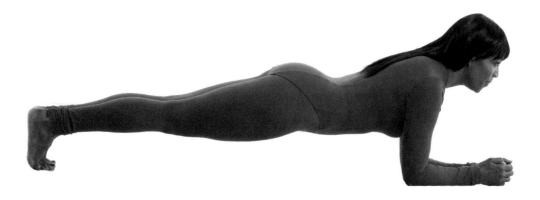

THE MOVE: Power Plank

continued »

YOU'LL FEEL IT: In your abs, back, glutes, and chest.

THE BODY-LOVE BENEFIT: Every woman should be able to hold her own weight, and this move demands that you do. It tightens and tones your "corset" muscles—the deepest abdominal muscles that hold you upright and naturally suck in your stomach—so you'll immediately improve your posture and feel more sure of yourself.

145

Holding that position, lift your right leg straight up as far as comfortably possible without arching your back, and then return to the starting position.

Repeat six times, and then switch to the opposite leg.

THE MOVE: Power Plank, *continued*

KACY'S COACHING TIPS: It's easy to "cheat" on this move by letting your belly sag toward the floor or arching your butt up toward the sky. To keep yourself honest, try placing a broomstick or a dowel on your back. If it rests on the back of your head, between your shoulders, and on your butt, you're arrow straight and doing it right.

Stand in the power position, feet wider than shoulder-width apart, with your toes turned out. Grasp the dowel so the right end is longer than the left. Hold it above your head, hands slightly wider than shoulder-width apart.

THE MOVE: Staff Side Bend

continued »

YOU'LL FEEL IT: In your obliques, abs, back, booty, legs, and shoulders.

THE BODY-LOVE BENEFIT: This is a graceful yet powerful move that will train your body to bend and be flexible while also being sturdy and strong, just like your spirit.

Fire your obliques and bend to the right, bending your knees into a wide plié and tapping the end of the dowel on the floor next to your right foot (or as close to it as possible while maintaining good form).

Return to the starting position. Complete a full set, and then switch sides.

THE MOVE: Staff Side Bend, *continued*

KACY'S COACHING TIPS: We don't spend a lot of time bending from side to side, so many women are inflexible through their obliques, which causes them to pitch forward or arch back while trying to perform this move. Your body should be completely straight as though you are bending between two sheets of glass. If you can't reach the floor right away, just go as far as you can but keep your form spot-on.

Stand in the power position, feet slightly apart. Place your left hand on your hip. Hold a staff or body bar in your right hand for support. The end of the bar should be positioned close to the toes of your right foot. Lift your right leg so it's bent at a 90-degree angle and even with your hip.

THE MOVE: Warrior II

continued »

YOU'LL FEEL IT: Lifting and shaping your glutes from the deepest inner muscles outward. It also hits your thighs and core.

THE BODY-LOVE BENEFIT: For most women, their butt is the final frontier. Once they finally see real firmness and shape back there, they start to believe they are capable

Swing your right leg back into a deep
lunge position so it is bent as close to
90 degrees as possible.

THE MOVE: Warrior II, *continued*

of absolutely anything. After a few weeks of this move, you'll take a peek back there
and believe!

KACY'S COACHING TIPS: This is a full lower-body move. Do not assist the movement
by using the staff to pull yourself in and out of the lunge position.

Keeping your right leg extended, straighten your left leg while you drag the toes of the right foot along the floor until they are about a foot behind your left heel and both legs are extended.

continued »

Immediately lean forward into an arabesque, bending your left knee slightly and fully extending your right leg, while lowering your torso until your body is parallel to the floor.

Return to the starting position, but don't pause; immediately flow into the next rep. For the first six, keep it slow, concentrating on getting all the parts of the move down correctly. Pick up the pace for the final six reps, flowing quickly and smoothly. Complete a full set, and then switch sides.

THE MOVE: Warrior II, *continued*

Stand in the power position with feet together, arms straight out in front of you and hands clasped. Lift your right leg out to the side. Keeping your foot flexed, immediately step into a side lunge.

THE MOVE: Inner Thigh Toner

continued »

YOU'LL FEEL IT: In that hard-to-reach inner thigh area, as well as your outer thighs and glutes.

THE BODY-LOVE BENEFIT: Strong, firm inner and outer thighs simply make your legs better able to walk fast, climb strong, and hold you up when you'd otherwise tire out. Jiggle-free thighs are also good for the spirit.

Return to the starting position, pulling your right foot slowly back to the left, lifting it up and keeping it off the floor the entire time.

THE MOVE: Inner Thigh Toner, *continued*

KACY'S COACHING TIPS: For the full toning impact of this move, squeeze your thigh muscles as hard as you can as you pull your lunging leg back to center. By keeping your working leg off the floor, you'll get a butt-busting benefit.

154

Without touching down, immediately go into the next rep.

Complete a full set, and then switch legs.

Stand in the power position. Lift your right knee up at 90 degrees straight in front of you, while softening your left leg. Position your arms in a "running" stance, with the left arm bent in front of you, left hand clasped in a loose fist in front of your left shoulder, and your right arm bent behind you with your hand in a loose fist behind your back.

THE MOVE: Running Goddess

YOU'LL FEEL IT: In your glutes, chest, core, and shoulders.

THE BODY-LOVE BENEFIT: This move is setting the stage for I Do. It's athletic yet amazingly graceful. Every time you perform it, you should feel a deeper connection being forged between your body and spirit.

All in one smooth move, bend forward about 45 degrees and swing your right leg back (keeping it bent) while switching arm positions, swinging the right out in front and the left one back. Allow your left leg to bend naturally.

Return to the starting position. Complete a full set, and then switch sides.

KACY'S COACHING TIPS: Stay loose! It's easy to get all tense while trying to stay balanced during this dynamic move. But it's 1,000 times harder if your fists are clenched and your shoulders are hunched up around your ears. Picture yourself like a long, lean, agile goddess running through the fields. Let it go, and let it flow.

Stand in the power position and hold 8- to 15-pound dumbbells down by your sides, palms facing back. Take a giant step back with your left leg, and bend your right knee. Keeping your back leg straight and balanced on the ball of your foot, drop your hips until your right thigh is parallel to the floor.

THE MOVE: NY Booty Lift

YOU'LL FEEL IT: In your butt!

THE BODY-LOVE BENEFIT: Your booty is the engine that drives you forward down the sidewalk, propels you up stairs, and helps you lift and carry heavy loads. When it's strong—and this move will make it stronger than you could ever imagine—there's no stopping you.

Keeping your back straight, bend forward from your hips and lower the weights to either side of your right foot.

Squeeze your glutes and raise back to the starting (lunge) position. Repeat the move for a full set, and then switch sides.

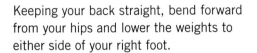

KACY'S COACHING TIPS: Your butt is guaranteed to burn, which can make some women lose good form and start lifting themselves out of the lunge position or trying to bend from the waist rather than the hips. Breathe deeply and work through the burn. Each rep will get a little easier.

Stand in the power position with feet close together, knees soft. Bend forward and bend knees slightly. Hold a dumbbell in each hand with your arms bent, elbows close to your body, and hands in front of you in loose fists as though you're holding the ends of an imaginary triceps pull-down rope.

THE MOVE: Power Press

YOU'LL FEEL IT: In the backs of your upper arms and shoulders.

THE BODY-LOVE BENEFIT: Your triceps are your "pressing" muscles—the ones you use to push overloaded grocery carts and hoist heavy loads overhead. When they're strong, you'll feel like you can move anything—even a mountain—that is in your way.

Squeeze your triceps and press your hands out to your sides and back behind you as far as possible, rotating your palms up toward the ceiling.

Squeeze your triceps a little harder in that position, hold for 1 second, and then bring the weights back to the starting position.

KACY'S COACHING TIPS: Keep your shoulders down and relaxed throughout the move. Don't allow tension to build in your neck and upper back.

Stand in the power position with feet close together, knees slightly bent. Hold a dumbbell in each hand, and keeping your elbows close to your sides, bend your arms so your forearms are extended straight out in front of your body at waist height, palms facing up.

THE MOVE: Fuel to the Fire

YOU'LL FEEL IT: Primarily in your biceps and to a lesser extent in your shoulders and chest.

THE BODY-LOVE BENEFIT: Like I told Julianne Moore, firm, curvy arms let powerful women embrace the world with that much more oomph.

Squeeze your right biceps and lift the weight up to your shoulder.

Lower back to the starting position, and immediately repeat the move with the left arm. Continue alternating for a full set to each side.

KACY'S COACHING TIPS: This is one move where I would advise going a little heavier. The weights should be heavy enough that it's challenging just to hold them in the starting position. (Hence the name. Your biceps should be firing even before you add the "fuel" of lifting the weights through the move.)

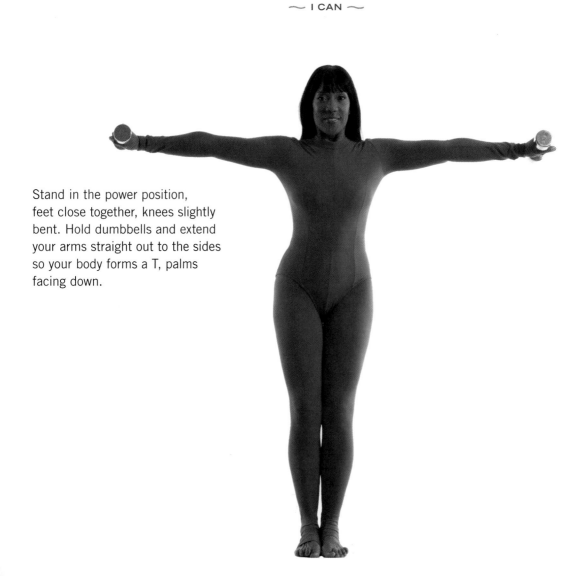

Stand in the power position, feet close together, knees slightly bent. Hold dumbbells and extend your arms straight out to the sides so your body forms a T, palms facing down.

THE MOVE: Open with Strength

YOU'LL FEEL IT: In your shoulders and chest.

THE BODY-LOVE BENEFIT: This move builds your upper body, giving you a sexy, formidable presence no one will be able to ignore.

164

Keeping your arms extended, squeeze your right pec and shoulder muscle, and swing your right arm forward until it's straight out in front of you.

Return to the starting position, and immediately repeat the move with the opposite arm. Continue alternating arms for a full set to each side.

KACY'S COACHING TIPS: Light weights are the way to go here. Even 8-pound dumbbells can feel like 30 pounds when you hold them out to your sides for more than a few seconds. You want to strengthen, not strain, your shoulders.

Woman Warrior Inspiration

~ *Nike* ~

Not the shoe company, but its namesake—the Greek goddess of victory—really did know how to "just do it." Her great power helped the gods seek victory over the gigantic, awesome Titans. But Nike was more than a goddess of military might; she was also the goddess of athletic achievement (hence the famous affiliations). She can help you overcome your obstacles and succeed as well. Embrace her and the spirit of female power, and you will discover victory—victory over the emotions and thoughts that have kept you trapped in your "old" body, blind to its inner strength and amazing potential. Whenever you feel stuck, as if nothing more can be done, call on Nike for enlightenment and encouragement. Imagine her standing by with the victory sash, cheering you on and ready to reward you for your efforts.

Remember to stretch. You can repeat the simple yet highly effective stretches on pages 70–78 in the I Am section.

9

Get Your Groove On

At this point, your body should be craving activity. You should know what it feels like to work hard, and you should have found a few activities—whether it's a new exercise class or power walking through the park—that you enjoy enough to work hard at. Now, before you give your body a chance to get bored, it's time to take it to the next level. Your cardio workouts during the I Can phase will reflect your emerging, powerful, and ever-curious spirit. Most important, they'll show you how to unload your physical energy in a way that lifts your spirit to the highest of highs.

Stay with me here. Using high-intensity exercise to elevate your spirit is something many people don't immediately understand. Too often they have the opposite perception—that exercise should leave them wiped out, spent. I have clients who come in and want me to "punish" them. I don't know what they've done wrong, and though I do appreciate their desire to work hard, I firmly feel that exercise should never be grueling. It should never beat you down. It should lift you up. The goal of I Can cardio is for you to feel a real lightness of being. You should smile (at least inside) when you do it. You should tune in to your movement and concentrate on playing a little while making it look graceful and pretty. You should feel strong, light, and ready to take on the world.

Of course, I don't expect you to conquer all that on your own. The I Can cardio workouts will help show you the way. I've included my signature jump-rope calisthenics, power plyometrics intervals, and another high-energy and revitalizing cardio workout. After just a few sessions, you'll find that this type of I Can interval training isn't just a tool to greater fitness; it's also a means to discovering your true potential.

Raise the Roof

You already know from reading through the I Am section that high-energy cardio burns tons of calories and fat. But scientists have recently discovered that this type of workout has benefits far beyond the obvious. Just a few minutes of high-intensity intervals can improve your general fitness as well as, if not better than, hours of more mellow effort.

It's true. Check this out. Canadian scientists took a small group of exercisers and divided them into two groups. One group did four to six full-throttle 30-second sprints on exercise bikes (they rested about 4 minutes between efforts) three days a week for two weeks. The second group also worked out three days a week for two weeks, only they pedaled at an easy pace for 90 minutes to two hours a pop. Guess what? Both groups came up with identical fitness gains. That's right. Both groups boosted their ability to use oxygen (a prime indicator of endurance) by about 30 percent. Both increased their number of *mitochondria*—those are your cells' fat-burning, fuel-making furnaces. And both saw a big rise in their number of fat-burning enzymes and muscle-buffering capacity (meaning they could burn more fat and exercise stronger and longer without feeling fried). The real-world payoff to this type of training is that you get fitter (and slimmer) faster. By raising your fitness ceiling so your body can tolerate and recover from hard efforts, you make all exercise feel easier. And the demands of day-to-day life? Suddenly they're a snap! Even better, your metabolism stays revved up about five times longer after an ass-kicking workout than after an easy one, so you also burn more fat and calories all day long.

That's just the physical stuff. I believe that hard physical effort also elevates your spirit by revealing your potential. When you see what your body is capable of, it's easier to believe in yourself in all areas of life. Intense exercise is also medically proven to make you more stress-resilient in your everyday life. Your body reads vigorous exercise as a really big stressor (a good one, but a stressor nonetheless). When you do it, your body floods your system with feel-good chemicals and artery-relaxing hormones to help you keep cool. After a while, your body learns how to respond more healthfully to all kinds of stressors, whether it's a jerk cutting you off in traffic or the 10th mile of a half-marathon. And exercise burns off toxic, stress-related hormones like adrenaline and cortisol, so you feel more relaxed and healthier in general.

That's not to say you should be out there taking yourself to the max every single time you lace up your shoes. You most definitely shouldn't! As you'll learn in the following chapter, your body makes its biggest gains when it's not working. So you need to take it easy some days too and give your muscles and energy systems a chance to recover and rebuild. It's the combination of hard work, easy efforts, and rest that will allow you to reach your fullest potential.

Energy Infusions

Confession time. As much as I pride myself on being a high-energy, highly self-motivated person, there are some days—when I've been running like a madwoman all over town seeing clients and having meetings and dealing with the headaches and hassles of big-city living—when the last thing I feel like doing is "walking my talk" and getting my butt to the gym, let alone banging out high-intensity intervals. If I'm truly tired, I'll take the day and either rest or go easy. But more often than not, I recognize that all I need is a little external boost to fan those internal fires. Here are some of the best ways I've found to kick-start a workout and throw my energy into high gear when I feel stalled out.

Roll Out Slow

On low-energy days, you really need to let your body warm up to the idea of working hard. So instead of going easy for just a minute or two, as many of you time-rushed women no doubt do, take at least five full minutes to warm up at half your usual speed. Warming up gradually raises the temperature in your muscles so they work more efficiently. It also gives you a chance to pick up momentum slowly and shake off those sluggish, stressed-out feelings. Studies show that even elite runners perform significantly better following a five-minute warm-up than when they spend little or no time getting up to speed. When you give your body a chance to acclimate to exercise, you feel physically, emotionally, and spiritually better, and you're able to go longer and perform better.

Get a Whiff of This

I'm a big believer in aromatherapy and the power the right scents can have on our senses. So it was no surprise to me that exercise researchers discovered that athletes ran faster during treadmill tests after sniffing some peppermint than when they ran scent-free or sniffed other, less-energizing scents. On those days when you just can't get going, try splashing a dash of peppermint oil on your workout shirt (at the very least, you'll smell good) or even popping a piece of peppermint gum (but spit it out before you really start moving). The stimulating aroma works to lift your mood so you feel like you're not working as hard as you really are.

Take It Outside

For me, nothing cures a case of "draggin' ass" better than a run through Central Park. Research shows that the rejuvenation I feel isn't just my active imagination. Exercising out in the elements has been proven to have a pronounced positive effect on your mental and physical state. The reason is negative ions. When oxygen molecules come in contact with moving air (like the wind), water (especially flowing water like a river or the ocean), and sunlight, they slough off electrically charged particles called negative ions. In humans, these buzzing molecular bits generate feelings of well-being, alertness, and mental peace and clarity—almost a Zen-like state! (That's why a beach vacation is so healing.)

In short, unless the only place you have to run or walk is along a noisy, polluted highway, it's hard *not* to be energized by an outdoor workout. And you don't just feel better, you perform better too. In a study of 15 runners, researchers found that the volunteers ran faster during a 5K running test where they had to give it their all when they did the test outdoors than when they performed the same test inside on the treadmill. Even more interesting, although the runners scored better times outdoors, their average heart rate wasn't any higher than when they ran the test on the treadmill. That means they were running faster without working harder, which makes going that extra mile all the easier.

Move to the Music

Okay, I saved the most obvious energizer for last. Have you ever walked into a fitness club and heard silence? Hell, no! Even the yoga room has some tunes pumped in. Listening to music can help you push harder and further while feeling like you're exerting less—just what you need on those low-energy days. In one recent study, exercisers who pedaled on exercise bikes "traveled" 11 percent farther when they got to spin along to tunes than when they were forced to pedal in pin-drop silence. Why? Lots of reasons. For one, music is a pleasant distraction. Part of your brain is preoccupied listening to the songs, maybe even singing along in your head, so you're less likely to think about how hard you're working. Music also lifts your mood, making you more likely to feel like doing a little more.

And here's an amazing side benefit. There's some pretty solid scientific evidence that banging out your intervals while rocking out to OutKast just may boost your brainpower too. No joke. In a study of more than 30 men and women, volunteers scored twice as well on a written test after working out to music than after they exercised in silence. Though the researchers aren't 100 percent sure why it worked, they speculate that exercise increases signal activity in your brain and that music somehow helps organize those signals so your brain works better. Either way, it's cool. Just remember, keep the earbuds out of your ears when you need to hear your surroundings to stay safe, such as when you're out in traffic or jogging someplace where there aren't lots and lots of people around.

Power Cardio

By now you should be getting the hang of how to do interval workouts. But like any type of exercise, you need to keep changing it up if you want to keep seeing results. I've included a few of my favorite I Can interval routines here.

One-Two Cardio Punch

This might be the simplest (though not the easiest) interval workout ever—and it's definitely one of the most effective. You can do it on the treadmill, on your favorite walking or running trail, on an exercise or real bike, or even in the pool.

∞ Warm up for five full minutes.
∞ Turn up your exertion level to defcon-5 on the Show It Love exertion scale (see page 84).

- Hold that intensity for one full minute.
- Lower your intensity to easy on the exertion scale.
- Recover at that level for one full minute.
- Repeat 10 times. Gradually work up to doing 15 to 20 one-minute efforts.
- Cool down two to three minutes and stretch.

The payoff of all this effort? Lab researchers found that compared to doing one 30-minute moderate-intensity run, runners who did 20 one-minute sprints as described here not only burned more calories while they ran but scorched more than twice as many calories in the hours following their workout as well.

Jump Master Fat Blaster

Hate cardio? Here's a 15-minute calorie-scorching, fat-blasting workout that'll get your heart pumping strong for 20 minutes. Because you're switching quickly from lower- to upper-body work, the time passes fast. Bonus: nothing delivers more bone-building bang for your exercise buck as jumping rope.

- Warm up for five full minutes.
- Jump rope for 30 seconds.
- Perform six push-ups.
- Stop in the up position on the final push-up and hold a plank position for 10 seconds.
- Repeat the entire sequence for six cycles.

Each week add 10 seconds of jump rope, 2 push-ups, and 10 seconds in the plank position, until you are performing one minute of jump rope, 12 push-ups, and 30 seconds of plank position.

Woman Warrior Inspiration

~ *Yemaya* ~

When you're joyfully and energetically moving your beautiful body through your I Can workouts, take a moment to give a nod to Yemaya, the mother of all living things and goddess of the ocean in Afro-Cuban mythology. Serving also as the patron deity of women—especially pregnant women—she is a strong, motherly protector and aims to lift the burden of sorrow from women who call to her. Her power and love stretch as deep and as far as the ocean itself, and her creed is "Do not be afraid to visit me in the depths." Not surprisingly, she is also a guardian for sailors and ensures safe passage to those traveling the seas under her watchful eye. Indeed, when I'm feeling low and lost at sea, I look to Yemaya and feel grounded once more.

Power Plyometrics Mix

Here's a quick way to work up a sweat without leaving your living room. When I need to bang out a quick cardio workout and burn off some stress (and calories), this is what I do.

- Warm up for five full minutes.
- Run in place, lifting your knees high for 30 seconds.
- Do jumping jacks for 30 seconds.
- Do Jump Squat Thrusts* for 30 seconds.
- Repeat the sequence 10 times.

*The Jump Squat Thrust is a high-octane move I developed just for this book. Start with a jump squat—squat down and jump straight into the air, thrusting your arms over your head. As you come down, plant your hands on the floor by your feet, then kick your legs straight back, so you're in a push-up position. Jump your feet back to your hands. Stand up, and repeat.

10

Rest, Recovery, and Regeneration

Sometimes the first thing I have to tell a client is *not* to exercise. When I first met model Anne V., for instance, she was an energetic, eager-to-please kid. She hadn't yet had her big break in the modeling world and was beating herself into the ground trying to get the body she wanted—strong, shapely, not too thin or too bulky. I had to say, "Don't exercise for two days. Give your body time to rest, recover, and get stronger. Give your head a rest too. Go have some fun."

She did. And that set the tone for how she would work out from there on—like an athlete. She'd go at it hard for a few days, then rest and let all that hard work sink in and give her spirit a chance to rejuvenate. Then we'd hit it again. Through that process, she learned how to work hard *and* enjoy her life. She came to embrace the process of working with her body and developed an inner sense of confidence and calm. Not too long after, she was gracing the pages of the 2005 *Sports Illustrated* swimsuit issue. Her pictures say it all. She's young, having fun, and in love with life. Chances are you're not a swimsuit model, but you can learn the same lessons.

Your Body Works When You Don't

Anyone who's ever trained for a marathon knows you are primed to perform your best after a period of rest. Why? Because hard training breaks your body down, and rest rebuilds it better than it was before. As a very extreme example, think of what happens when you break a bone, like your arm. Initially the impact and the fracture weaken the bone, and you have to give it rest so it can "knit," or mend. If you check out the X-ray once it's healed, however, you'll see that the spot where the break was is actually stronger than the rest of the bone. Your body, in its wisdom, always tries to keep you one step ahead of the game, making you strong enough to meet whatever challenges it thinks you might face. But if all you do is work it, work it, work it, you'll never give it the opportunity to fully improve. Instead, you create a state of chronic stress, where you not only don't get any stronger because you're constantly breaking your muscles down, but your body is so out of whack and screaming for help that you end up fatigued, cranky, and hungry. Then there's a good chance that all your hard work will end up in weight gain, not loss.

Honestly, I feel that the lack of true recovery and regeneration is one of the reasons America is one of the most obese countries in the world and why so many people fall out of their routines. They're burned out! Most of us are terrible workaholics, and we apply that same "must-do" mentality to our fitness programs. Well, your body is the boss, and it doesn't work that way. You cannot beat yourself into top form. You cannot be in the gym doing the same thing every single day and expect to make progress, no matter how hard you work or how dedicated you are. You have to ebb and flow and train like the athlete inside.

That's what I Can is all about. It's believing in your ability to challenge yourself, work hard, and go for it, while also believing in honoring your body and giving it what it needs to be its best. And the thing that is most often overlooked is rest.

The Three Rs

Before you think of turning one more page toward I Do—the final and most physically vigorous part of the Show It Love system—I want you to commit these three Rs to memory: rest, recovery, and regeneration. Learn them and live them.

Rest

Rest is just that, physical rest that includes chilling out with some friends and a great movie, as well as actual sleep. Let's talk about physical rest first. Once you hit full stride with the Show It Love system, you'll be working out with either strength training or cardio routines six days a week. Sometimes you'll be exercising twice a day. I expect you to take one day where you do nothing more physically demanding than window-shopping, walking the dog, or taking a leisurely bike ride through town. Your heart shouldn't be pounding. You shouldn't be sweating. Your muscles shouldn't be burning. That's how you know that you are allowing your body the time to regroup.

The second, and infinitely more important, thing for most women is sleep! Without enough sleep, your body goes into distress mode, and because it senses something is terribly amiss in your life, it starts storing up fat just in case you need extra energy to burn. Given that, it's little wonder that Columbia University researchers recently found that people who get just five hours of shut-eye a night are 50 percent more likely to be overweight or obese than those who shut down for a solid seven to nine hours of slumber every night. Even those who got six hours (fess up, that's you many nights, right?) were still 25 percent more likely to be overweight than their well-rested peers.

The more active you are, the more critical sleep becomes. While you're snoozing, your body rechannels every ounce of your usual waking energy into repairing muscle fibers, mopping up metabolic waste, and fully processing all the physical input and mental information you've poured into it during the day. Deep rapid-eye movement (REM) sleep—the kind where your eyes are darting beneath your lids and your mind is dreaming—is particularly important, because that's when your muscles are at their most relaxed. I know you're not going to get the recommended eight hours of sleep every night, but I bet you can get seven. If you get up at 6:00, that means going to bed at 11:00—not so bad. That gives you time to unwind, watch your favorite shows, and have a little quiet (or better yet, sexy) time before drifting off to sleep.

Recovery

Recovery is different from rest. While rest is mostly inactive, recovery is an active process. In fact, recovery happens every time you slow down between intervals and take a breath between strength training sets. It's the act of delivering nutrient-dense, oxygen-rich blood to your needy organs and muscles. For optimum muscle repair, you'll need to designate one or two cardio workouts a week to active recovery.

What you do after and between workouts also can speed up (or slow down) the recovery process. Primary on that list is what you eat and when you eat it. After a hard workout, your fuel stores are tapped out. Your muscles need fuel to repair, so you have to eat. (Notice I said after a *hard workout*. If you've just taken your pooch around the block, you don't need a recovery snack.) Research shows that by eating a small carbohydrate-and-protein snack within 20 to 30 minutes of a tough effort, you can refuel and repair your muscles many times faster than if you wait until your next meal. What's more, you're less likely to feel famished and overeat later on if you replenish your system with just a little something right away. It can be as simple as a small glass of chocolate skim or soy milk, or a half-slice of whole wheat bread with a little peanut butter.

Since our bodies are mostly water, it's also important to replace the fluids we sweat out. I carry a big bottle of water with me everywhere I go, so I'm sure to start and finish my workouts well hydrated. I suggest you do the same. When you're dehydrated, it's harder for your muscles to work properly, and your performance can suffer by up to 25 percent. Without enough fluid, your connective tissues around your joints dry up, leaving you feeling stiff and sore. And dehydration most definitely slows down recovery. Sports nutritionists say that active people should try to drink at least half their body weight in ounces of fluid. That means a 140-pound woman should try to drink nine cups a day. Though coffee and juices do count, get as much of your fluid intake from plain, clear water as possible. It's good for your skin, muscles, and digestive tract, as well as exercise recovery.

Finally, you've got to feed your muscles right if you want them to mend fast. Concentrate on free radical–fighting, antioxidant-rich fruits and vegetables. Vigorous exercise generates cell-damaging free radicals, and although your body generates its own natural antioxidants to fight them, it doesn't hurt to give it a little help in the form of healing nutrients like vitamins C and E and beta-carotene. The fresher and more colorful the produce, the better.

Regeneration

Regeneration is recovery of the mind and spirit. It can come in the form of a week off from working out, a weekend away from home, or even something as simple as a change in routine (like signing up for a new dance class). You know you're feeling regenerated when you're happy, maybe even a little juiced, about working out. For me, regeneration comes from connecting with people I love and meditating on my goals in life. It renews my sense of purpose and leaves me feeling grateful for my body and eager to get out there and honor it. For you, it may be learning a new sport like golf or tennis.

This much I can tell you for sure. The opposite of regeneration is burnout. So if you're walking around cursing your workouts and feeling mentally and spiritually spent, regenerating is exactly what you need. Start simple— change your workout. Sometimes that's all it takes to discover you really do like exercise; you're just sick of the StairMaster. If that doesn't work, play hooky for a day and go shopping. Chances are you just need a quick recharge to feel ready to roll again.

As you get better at listening to your body and responding to what it needs, you'll automatically know when it's time to go for it mentally and/or physically and when it's time to chill. In the meantime, I take the guesswork out of it for you in the exercise programs and workout logs at the end of each section. You'll find rest and recovery days built in. I also recommend that every month or so you pull back and reduce the volume of your workouts to let your body do some deep-down regeneration before turning it back up to 10. It's like the turtle and the hare. You'll get there faster if you don't burn yourself out.

Total Body Care

It should go without saying that every little thing you do contributes to your recovery and general well-being when you're working out and getting fit. But people never cease to surprise me. I have clients come in in terrible shape. On paper, it looks like they're doing everything right. They're following their routines to the letter, taking rest days, doing what they're supposed to do. Then I dig a little deeper and find out that they're going through a divorce, or it's the holidays and they've been drinking three martinis every night for the past week. So I have to say, "Look, stress is stress. If you're experiencing stress, whether it's from dumping too many toxins into your liver or cranking 24/7 on the job, your body is going to need extra recovery." That doesn't necessarily give you a free pass from working out. But it does mean that you can't expect to be able to push your body hard and have it bounce back as quickly as you've come to expect.

If you are burning the candle at both ends, you can help minimize the toll and speed recovery by giving yourself a little extra TLC. I like the following methods:

Woman Warrior Inspiration

~ *Isis* ~

In ancient Egypt, Isis was the goddess of health, healing, and immortality. She had incredible powers of magic and could command all living things at will. She could remove poison from any person's body and could heal all wounds. Her most famous feat was reassembling and bringing back to life her beloved Osiris after he was slain, dismembered, and scattered by her jealous brother. She reassembled him, giving him a golden penis, and later conceived and gave birth to the sun god Horus. For that, Isis became known as the ultimate goddess of renewal and mothering. She is the one to think of when you're feeling tapped out mentally and physically. She stands to remind us that we need to mother, or nurture, ourselves if we hope to heal and progress. By studying Isis, you can learn that power comes not just from strength, wisdom, and power (no matter how great) but also from knowledge, rest, and regeneration.

- **Massage.** My cowriter, Selene, swears by a hot stone massage to settle her runaway stress and set her back on track. I say, whatever works, whether it's a rubdown from your honey or a full spa treatment. Physically flushing your muscles while you quiet your mind and calm your nerves definitely quells the draining effects of stress and quickens recovery.
- **Aromatherapy.** Lavender is a great place to start (it's a classic relaxation herb) and chamomile and lavender together are wonderfully soothing. Lemon and sage is also a calming combination. Candles in these scents may be tough to find, so experiment. Buy a few essential oils and drip them into the pool of wax in an ordinary store-bought jar candle.
- **Meditation.** Light some candles, dim the lights, sit quietly, and still your mind. Let anxious thoughts float through and keep right on going. Breathe deeply and slowly. You'll find that it's physically impossible to feel anxious and out of control when you're meditating. I recommend it for a daily dose of regeneration.

I Can Milestones

Are You Ready to Take It to the Top?

You've reached the last few pages of I Can, but are you ready for the final chapter in your fitness journey? The spiritual empowerment that comes with I Can is possibly the most important step to achieving lifelong fitness (and even happiness), so don't rush it! You're ready to move forward only when your thoughts are filled with your potential, not wrapped up in your self-perceived shortcomings; when you not only embrace new challenges but go out searching for them; and when you're constantly on the hunt for new ways to be active and eat healthfully, rather than inventing excuses for skipping workouts and trashing your body with junk food.

Here are some questions to measure your progress in the I Can portion of the Show It Love program. You should proceed to I Do when, in your heart of hearts, you can answer the following questions positively and truthfully:

1 **Spend a moment taking inventory of your personal power. As you walk down the street, how do you feel?**
- **a.** I find myself beset by some doubts and body worries.
- **b.** I feel a growing confidence and power.
- **c.** I experience buoyancy that can come only from true, new confidence.

2 **How do you eat on an average evening?**
- **a.** I eat very small meals so I don't break my diet.
- **b.** I find myself able to enjoy my favorite foods in appropriate portions, keeping a balanced food intake.
- **c.** I eat healthfully but fully enjoy a taste of my favorite sensual foods.

3 **When you see a woman with a body you admire, how do you react?**

    a. I take inventory and feel that I'm not making enough progress.

    b. I find myself appreciating my own physical gifts.

    c. I feel proud of my accomplishments and curious about how she got such incredible legs/thighs/arms.

4 **Imagine an actress who has the absolutely perfect butt. What are you thinking?**

    a. I'll never feel good unless I get a body like hers.

    b. I'll never have a butt like that no matter what I do.

    c. I want that ass. I'm going to figure out how to get it, and I will get it.

5 **What goals have you set for yourself lately?**

    a. I haven't gotten to that yet.

    b. I've pledged to get into a size 10 by summer.

    c. I've signed up for my first 10K.

6 **The last time you blew off a workout, what was your reason?**

    a. I played hooky to do some shopping, but I did feel guilty.

    b. I was sincerely tired from a stressful day, but I did take a little walk for fresh air and got right back to it the next day.

    c. I was laid up in bed with the flu wishing I could get up and do something.

7 **How have your friends acted toward you lately?**

    a. They've said next to nothing new or unusual.

    b. They asked if I've cut my hair recently.

    c. They're looking at me in a completely new way, and I'm looking right back.

If your answers are mostly a, hang back and continue to work on I Am. If they're mostly b, move on gradually but keep spending a few days a week on I Am exercises. If they're mostly c, leap into I Do with power and feeling.

I Can Workout Log

By this point, exercise should be a habit and so should keeping your workout log. Faithfully recording your daily progress helps you keep track of where you are and, more important, how far you've come.

Your first week of I Can should look like this:

MONDAY	TUESDAY	WEDNESDAY	THURSDAY	FRIDAY	SATURDAY	SUNDAY
Woman Warrior, 3 sets Stretches	Cardio, 30–40 minutes or 20 minutes high-intensity intervals (e.g., One-Two Cardio Punch, p. 172)	Woman Warrior, 3 sets Stretches	Cardio, 30–40 minutes or 20 minutes high-intensity intervals (e.g., Jump Master Fat Blaster, p. 173)	Woman Warrior, 3 sets Stretches	Cardio, 30–40 minutes or 20 minutes high-intensity intervals (e.g., Power Plyometrics Mix, p. 174)	Off

Use the log sheet on the next page to track your progress.

I Can Log Sheet

THE MOVE	NUMBER OF SETS/ NUMBER OF REPS	I FELT . . .
Creative Curl	_____	_____
Power Plank	_____	_____
Staff Side Bend	_____	_____
Warrior II	_____	_____
Inner Thigh Toner	_____	_____
Running Goddess	_____	_____
NY Booty Lift	_____	_____
Power Press	_____	_____
Fuel to the Fire	_____	_____
Open with Strength	_____	_____

THE CARDIO	NUMBER OF MINUTES	I FELT . . .
One-Two Cardio Punch	_____	_____
Jump Master Fat Blaster	_____	_____
Power Plyometrics Mix	_____	_____
Other _____	_____	_____

PART 3

I Do

"WHAT do you do?" How many times

have you been asked that question? At

parties, at family gatherings, whenever you

meet someone new, the first words out of the

person's mouth after "hello" are "What do

you do?" We are largely defined not just by

who we are (I Am) but by what we do (I Do).

Sure, part of that is your career—the work

you do to buy food and keep the lights on. But by now a growing part of what you do should be defined by movement, as in, "I *do* 10Ks"; "I *do* Woman Warrior exercises"; and "I *do* the most amazing things with my body!"

That's what the final section of the Show It Love journey is all about—reaching your physical potential. It's where we take your rock-solid emotional and spiritual foundation and start carving beautiful lines. Unlike many other fitness programs that try to tackle this part first (and only this part), I save it for last. I've learned from 25 years of experience that though you can (and I do) firm and tighten someone's belly and thighs in a few weeks, unless you also help them wash away the emotional self-hate and dump the spiritual baggage, they won't reach and definitely won't maintain the body of their dreams. Once they reach I Do, my clients are gushing about the reflection in the mirror as well as the transformation inside their skin. You will be too.

The I Do phase of the Show It Love system emphasizes an approach that caters to your most physical self, from strengthening moves worthy of an elite athlete (and very often a movie star playing one on the big screen) to diet dos and don'ts for fueling a body in motion. You're going to have to push yourself out of your comfort zone. I'm going to ask you to dip your toes into unfamiliar and sometimes intimidating waters. You're going to achieve physical prowess—and emotional and spiritual confidence—you never thought possible.

With that as my goal, I specially designed the I Do sequence of strengthening exercises to tap into every aspect of your physicality. From the flying Heel-Click Plié to the strong, grounded Goddess, you'll feel every muscle fire up to keep your body flying and flowing. When I say, "Do you [*fill in your name*] accept the challenges that lie before you to leap and soar until the end of your days?" I expect you to raise your fist and shout, "I do!"

In the final analysis, the I Do section is simply a celebration of self, and although that party is happening on the outside, all the preparation has been done on the inside. Successfully complete this section and you'll be utterly undaunted by any challenge life throws your way. You'll just jump over it (with a little side kick for flair) and keep right on rocking and rolling. In the I Do section, you will find:

∞ **Self-training tools.** Congratulations, you're a personal trainer! Okay, maybe not, but damn close, at least for yourself. In this final section of *The Show It Love Workout*, I let go of your hand and kick you out of the nest. Ultimately, I want you to be able to come up with your own ass-kicking exercise routines so you can stay juiced up to hit the gym and keep the results coming. In the pages that follow, you'll find a little how-to advice. You'll also find my personal suggestions for keeping an exercise journal, because I believe nothing is as inspiring as your own written words.

∞ **Athletic eats.** You're an athlete. Now it's time to start eating like one. As you push yourself ever harder, you'll find that the fuel you feed your muscles is increasingly important. Here I share the secrets of top sports nutritionists and the athletes they train. You won't just learn what to eat but, more important, when to eat it. You won't believe the difference it makes.

∞ **Woman Warrior series 3.** I Do includes the final installment of my signature Warrior exercise series, which is the ultimate blend of athleticism, grace, and sheer fun. These moves are designed to really show off what your brand-new booty can do. You'll jump. You'll kick. You'll lift, sweep, and swing. As a reward, you'll see what you've been waiting for: sleek, sexy calves; lean, toned thighs; sweet, smooth lines running down your belly; that killer dimple on the side of your butt. You've set the stage. I Do will help you get it done.

On your mark. Get set. Say, "I do!"

11

Fuel like a Ferrari

One of my favorite clients of all time was a Ferrari dealer and enthusiast named Roffredo Gaetani, from the Royal Family of Italy, who, sadly, passed away in a car crash during the writing of this book. This man had been a thespian, a boxer, and a successful business owner. At 50-something, he could definitely afford to let himself slide. But he was always among my most physically fit clients. Why? He was extremely disciplined about what he put in his body. He knew that what he ate would profoundly affect how well he skied, boxed, and performed in the gym. Just as you wouldn't put cheap gas in the cars he sold and loved, you shouldn't put junk in your body if you want to be a top performer.

Now that you have reconciled your emotional relationship with food and allowed yourself to enjoy meals that soothe the soul, we will move on to the nuts and bolts of designing a diet for high physical performance. Keep in mind also that exercise nutrition is a lifelong work in progress. I can give you all the tips I know on fueling your muscles for performance and recovery, but ultimately it's a matter of trial and error. Some of my clients have iron stomachs and can exercise right after eating pancakes and eggs. Others need a couple of hours to digest after eating if they don't want to go green on the elliptical machine. Take this advice as a guideline and experiment to find the right fueling strategy for you.

Top Off Your Tank

Many of my clients are trying to lose weight, so they immediately balk when I suggest they have a small snack before they work out. But at the I Do exercise level, a little fuel for your fire will help you lose more weight in the long run than if you drive it on empty.

How? Simple. Your muscles rely on the carbs you eat daily to fuel your workouts. Let's say you haven't eaten since breakfast, so you snack on a 100-calorie banana an hour or so before you hit the gym at lunch. Those 25 to 30 grams of carbs (as well as important muscle-function minerals like potassium) will top off your muscle glycogen (stored fuel) stores and leave you raring to go. So when you get to the club, you can bang out 30 minutes of high-quality cardio followed by your Woman Warrior routine and scorch off about 600 calories—almost one-third of a day's worth.

Now let's suppose you skip the snack and hit the club hungry instead. Twenty minutes into your interval workout, you start to feel a little lightheaded, so you slow down and cut it short. Still a little weak, you do just two sets of your strength moves instead of three. In the end, you burn 400 (maybe 500) calories because you weren't properly fueled. Without adequate carbs on board, your body may also start eating into your muscle stores to get the work done. Remember, muscle is your metabolic gold mine. It keeps your calorie burn set to high, so you want to preserve every ounce. Finally, working out on empty leaves you more likely to feel ravenous when you're done, which makes it all too easy to go back home or to the office and eat twice as much as you would normally. This is how women who are working out to lose weight actually end up packing it on instead. Remember, you're here to honor your body and give it what it needs to do the work you're asking of it, not starve it and try to whip it into the shape you want. Always Show It Love.

If you want your body to perform its best, make sure there's a little something in your system, especially if it's been more than three hours since your last meal. It shouldn't be anything heavy that'll weigh you down or upset your stomach. Try a glass of Gatorade or other sports drink, a piece of fruit, or a small energy bar. (Luna Bars are perfect. They're just over 100 calories; easy to digest; and made with delicious, organic ingredients.) Avoid anything with a lot of fat, like nut butters and cheese, or high-fiber foods, like bran muffins, because they all slow digestion and could come back (literally) to haunt you as you turn up the pace on the treadmill.

How much time you need to allow yourself for digestion is a matter of personal preference and biology, but generally speaking, I allow three hours after a big meal (like a full soup-and-sandwich lunch); two to three hours after a small meal (a bowl of cereal or a piece of fruit); and an hour or less for a small snack (yogurt or an energy bar), depending on what type of workout I'm doing. High-intensity exercise will shunt more blood away from your digestive system, so it's better to err on the lighter side before heavy workouts. Ditto for running and jumping-type exercises that physically jostle your stomach around. General strength workouts and activities like bike riding and walking are more forgiving, so you can be a little less cautious about your food selections.

It should go without saying (but I'm going to say it anyway) that if you're just going out for a walk in the park, you don't need to be chugging Gatorade and chowing on sports bars. Just grab a few sips of water off your bottle to be sure you're hydrated and head out the door. Leave the more serious fueling for your more concerted efforts.

Eating for Endurance

If you are well nourished going into your workouts, you aren't going to need any special snacks or sports fuels while you exercise. But my hope is that by this point you're inspired to push your physical limits with a larger challenge like a triathlon, a charity bike ride, or a 10K run. If/when you do, you'll definitely need to learn to eat on the run!

This isn't a marathon training guide, so I won't devote too much space to hard-core sports nutrition. But I will touch on a few of the most important fueling facts to keep in mind when you're taking your body the distance.

- **Train your gut.** This is the most important rule to remember. Your digestive system needs to be trained just like your muscular and cardiovascular systems. That is, don't expect it to do everything perfectly the first time out. If you've never asked your body to digest during exercise, it may not respond very well the first few times you throw down some fig bars. But trust me on this. Just like your heart and muscles step up to the challenge as you train them, so will your stomach. You just have to start slow and experiment a little. Eventually it will come to crave the extra energy that a well-timed snack can provide during long, hard efforts.
- **Eat at 90.** Your muscles have about 1,500 calories of stored fuel in them, which means if you're out running or riding with any kind of intensity, you'll be on fumes in about two hours. Don't wait until you're ready to pass out to replenish yourself (remember, fuel helps you stay fast, which ultimately burns more calories). Have a bite of a bar or some sports drink 90 minutes into a long workout to give your body the energy to finish strong.
- **Drink up.** You can work up a big sweat even during short workouts if you're turning up the intensity. In a warm gym environment or on a hot day outside, you can easily lose up to a quart of sweat. When you lose fluid, your blood thickens and is harder for your heart to pump, which slows you down and fatigues you faster. Even slight dehydration can also leave you headachy long

after your workout's done. Stash a water bottle in your gym bag to have on hand and help you stay hydrated.

- **Be playful.** With all the precisely engineered sports nutrition products on the market, you would be blown away by what some professional- and elite-level athletes rely on to get them through Ironman, marathons, and other grueling events. Crack open their snack bags and you'll find gummy bears, jelly beans, frozen Snickers bars, animal crackers, hard candy, Twizzlers, oatmeal cookies, and cold pasta. No joke! That's because they know that when the going gets tough and they feel like throwing in the towel, a banana or another PowerBar isn't necessarily going to inspire them to continue. But a few malted milk balls might lift their spirits (and their blood sugar) just enough to see them through to the finish line. It's a good reminder that even when you're working on the very physical level, it's important to feed your emotional self as well.

Calories Count

Unless you live underground, you've heard that to lose weight you need to cut calories. But research shows that the vast majority of us—including many nutritionists—don't have a clue how many calories we're actually supposed to eat every day. This is one of those simple questions with a lot of very complex answers. How many calories your body uses depends on your sex, your activity level, your muscle and bone structure, your genetics, and dozens of other factors. So let's keep it as simple as possible and work with ballpark figures. Here's one of my favorite formulas (based on the Harris-Benedict equation, a more complex formula that determines resting metabolism and calories burned during activity):

- Multiply your current weight by 13 to 14 if you are a lightly to moderately active woman—meaning you exercise 30 to 45 minutes three or four days a week (which you *definitely* should be if you're following the Show It Love system). For a 140-pound woman, that's 1,820 to 1,960 calories a day.
- Multiply your weight by 15 to 16 if you are very active—meaning you work out 45 to 60 minutes most days a week (this is where most women following this program will fall). For a 140-pound woman, that's 2,100 to 2,240 calories a day.

The number you come up with is how many calories you need to maintain your current weight. To lose weight, shave off 200 to 500 calories from your daily intake, while also turning up your exercise time and/or intensity; you'll shed 1 to 2 pounds a week. To keep from feeling deprived or hungry, plan your eating as described in this chapter. Eat a little to fuel your workouts. Recover with a healthy meal afterward. And don't go into exercise sessions hungry; that makes you more likely to overeat.

12

Woman Warrior Series 3

It's Time to Fly

This book is custom-tailored to women, but the exercises are good for every body (and mind). Case in point: Lenny Kravitz has always had that high, firm butt we caught an eyeful of in the sexy video for "Again." I can't take credit for that beautiful booty. But I can take credit for changing his mind about what it takes to be a rock-solid rock star. (Just as I hope I'm changing your mind about what it takes to be a powerful, successful, beautiful woman.)

Lenny came to me because he loved the rock-and-roll life and wanted to have the strength and stamina to rock like the Stones well into his 50s and 60s. He wasn't just looking for ripped abs; he wanted to be strong and centered and be able to bang it out for a full show night after night without depleting under the demands of performing on stage.

During our first appointment, Lenny, like so many men (and even some women), was all about the hard-core pump. Other trainers had sold him the same old bill of goods that to make muscles, you need to grab the 50-pound dumbbells and get thrashing. I explained that we weren't going to attack his body or bash it with big, heavy weights and that sculpting is a delicate job. It's like creating a statue—you need to do fine, intricate work to make it pretty.

He smiled and said, "Oh, you do that Michelangelo shit, huh?" You'd better believe it, honey. And like Michelangelo, I know what it takes to carve a masterpiece. As we aired it out with power squats and jumps, Lenny saw a total transformation. Now he knows what he needs to do to keep rocking. Though he may work with other trainers as he travels through his career, he'll never let someone attack his body again. They'll have to come at it with some love.

This section focuses on sheer power and beauty with the I Do Woman Warrior series—the baddest moves of the bunch for building your best body ever. You'll also find more detailed exercise plans and logs, tips for avoiding and treating injury, and advice for keeping the progress coming. Let's go for it!

A Strong Vessel

We've just spent a lot of time exploring and working on your emotional and spiritual self. Many times along this Show It Love journey, I've told you to put aside all those purely body-focused thoughts while we worked on issues that were much more than skin-deep. But just because I believe in training from the inside out, it doesn't mean I don't appreciate the importance of the physical self. Far from it. Your body is the vessel that carries your spirit. Nothing could be more important. Once you've built a powerful emotional and spiritual core, you naturally want a strong, beautiful vessel to take it out into the world. That's what I Do is all about.

The major change you'll notice between the I Can moves from the last section and the I Do moves you're about to try is athleticism. My signature I Do moves tap into and pull out the inner athlete in everyone. You'll be pressing and leaping and moving your beautiful body with precision, power, and control. The foundation of many of the moves is the same as in earlier chapters, as you'll see with Warrior III; we just pump up the performance to really make your muscles pop. As before, you may be a little sore after the first few rounds of I Do workouts. But it'll be a good sore that soon subsides as your body rises to this new set of challenges.

Think of I Am, I Can, and I Do coming together here as the "perfect storm" of self-actualization. The stronger your physical self, the more energy you have and the more confidence you feel as you stare yourself square in the eye in the mirror every morning. That, in turn, enables you to go out and engage the world more completely and really go for what you want! I see it with my clients time and time again. By the time we get through I Do, they are rock stars in their own right. They know who they are, they know what they want, and they have the physical oomph to go out and fight for it day after day. The best part is that I know it's a transformation that'll stick, because it started in their hearts.

Protect as You Push

Your body is the only machine that lasts longer and performs better the more you use it. Study after study confirms that so much of what we chalk up to "getting old," whether it's creaky joints or a forgetful mind, is really a matter of our physical parts getting rusty from neglect. When you challenge your body the way you will in I Do, you lubricate your joints and strengthen your muscles and tendons, staving off arthritis. You strengthen your cardiovascular system, keeping heart disease at bay. You burn off stress hormones and bolster your immunity to fend off infections and disease, including many forms of cancer. You are undoubtedly healthier when you move more.

I would be remiss, however, if I didn't point out the one obvious risk: injury. When you're out there week after week challenging your body and pushing it to new heights, you do increase your chances of getting hurt, whether it's a random muscle strain or joint pain. *This in no way should discourage you from exercising!* The benefits of activity far outshine the hazards, which are still fairly low. But the risks are there, so let's minimize them by playing it smart.

As you saw in Chapter 10, you can avoid the vast majority of exercise-related aches and pains with the right amount of rest and by being mindful about eating well, warming up, and stretching. For the random twisted ankle or muscle twinge that sneaks through, show your body some extra love with the following steps.

Evaluate It

If I didn't exercise every time I felt a little sore here or there, I'd be in a different profession. Everyone, whether active or not, experiences some achiness now and then. The important thing for you to do, as an active person, is figure out whether it's something serious. The easiest way to tell is to pay attention to your pain. Is it sharp or dull? Is it in a joint or a muscle? Does it get worse with movement, or does it fade away as you get going? Generally speaking, dull pain that disappears with your warm-up isn't due to a show-stopping injury; it's probably the result of some tightness or microtrauma that hasn't fully healed. Likewise, you may occasionally land wrong and feel a twinge in your ankle or knee that resolves quickly as you walk it off. In both of these situations, you can move gently through the discomfort, but be sure to be extravigilant about your stretching and rest to make sure the hurt resolves itself without getting worse.

If you feel sharp pain anywhere, especially in a joint like your knee or ankle, that's your body telling you to stop. Other signs of an injury are swelling, pain when you press on the spot, and limited range of motion in that area. Those types of injuries can happen suddenly—you're running along, your foot lands wrong, you feel a pop and go, "Yow!" (If the pain and the swelling are downright crippling, especially if you also feel a little nauseous at the time of injury, bypass the next step and see a doctor ASAP to rule out a fracture or serious tear.) Injuries can also happen over time, when you've been running along for weeks with no problem, then one day start feeling a sharp stabbing in the side of your knee or in your Achilles tendon. If that's the kind of pain you're facing, go to the next step.

Try MICE

No, that's not a typo. I mean MICE, not RICE, the old standby for treating sports injuries. Docs used to preach rest, ice, compression, and elevation. But I swapped *motion* for *rest* because studies show that you heal faster when you keep your blood flowing. Obviously you shouldn't be stressing the injured area, but keep moving any way you can. If the injured spot hurts only when you put weight on it, try swimming. If the pain is in your shoulder, ride an exercise bike. This type of cross training not only boosts the circulation you need to mend, but it also lets you maintain aerobic fitness and get back to your usual routine sooner once you're healed.

Be sure to ice the injury twice a day, if possible. You don't need a fancy ice pack; a bag of frozen peas will do. Wrap it in a paper towel and place it on the area for 15 minutes or so. You can keep swelling down during the day by wrapping the injury with an Ace (compression) bandage and keeping it elevated (if it's a lower extremity) as much as possible. Most soft tissue injuries, like strains and sprains, will heal in a couple of weeks with a little MICE.

For pain around a joint, stretch the muscles surrounding that joint several times a day. Often, tightness in connective tissue, such as your Achilles tendon or iliotibial band (connective tissue running from your hip to your knee), can pull on a joint, causing pain. Check out the stretches on pages 70–78 to resolve and protect yourself from this type of injury. Most pain should subside in about two to four weeks if you follow this advice. If you feel no relief after a week or so, move on to the next step.

See a Professional

Injuries should make gradual, steady improvement. If you're still wincing after giving yours some rest, it's time to call the doctor. Your best bet is to head straight to a sports doc like an orthopedist or physiatrist who specializes in treating sports-related injuries. They'll run the necessary tests to diagnose the problem and give you an action plan to get you back on your feet again. Once you're well, move on to the final, and maybe most important, step.

Keep It from Coming Back

It's trite but true that prevention is your best medicine. If your sport-specific stretches helped heal your hurt, they'll also keep it from making a repeat performance, so keep them up. Likewise, it's not a bad idea to ice your knees after an especially long day on the bike or if you're marathon training; it keeps the inflammation down and allows the area to recover more quickly and completely. (Check out any elite athlete after a competition and you'll see him or her practically swimming in ice.)

Finally, be smart. Replace your running shoes every six months to cushion your joints; be especially careful on wet, slippery days; and always, always, always warm up before high-intensity exercise. Treat your body right, and it'll reward you with ouch-free performance for years to come.

The I Do Woman Warrior Moves: Unleash Your Inner Athlete

"Man, can I shape a butt!" That's what's going through my head so often as I stand behind my clients as they're banging out these powerful I Do moves. It's a great feeling to see their muscles shine through as their spirit soars. Even more satisfying is watching them put those finely tuned muscles into action. Whether I'm staring in awe at the silver screen while Kirsten Dunst swings through Gotham in the latest installment of *Spider-Man* or watching a client tilt the treadmill up to 10 for the first time, I get such satisfaction out of seeing strong bodies in full motion. That's what these athletic moves will do for you: sculpt, strengthen, and send you soaring.

Because many of the I Do moves have a plyometric (jumping) element, they are especially powerful for putting the finishing sculpting touches on all those tough-to-tone spots. When you leap and jump, you first stretch your muscle (like you're getting ready to fire a rubber band), then you spring into action. That increased range of motion, movement speed, and workload really tap into your type II fast-twitch muscle fibers. These are the full, shapely fibers that make Olympic sprinters look like Greek gods, and they're the first ones to start atrophying from disuse in all of us mere mortals. Well, the I Do moves will guarantee that yours don't wither away.

Speaking of muscles and performance, I urge you to really think about yourself as an athlete as you're performing these moves. Don't just do them—*perform* them. Make them fluid. Make them pretty. Go for flourish and grace. Pretend I'm standing there by your side and try to impress me with how much energy you pour into every rep. As you progress through this workout, it should feel like a marriage of effort and effortlessness as the goddess and the warrior merge together and you realize your full potential. The belief is there. The motivation is there. The strength is there. Now you're pulling it all together and really doing it!

At the risk of sounding like a broken record, expect to be a little sore the first few days from turning up the burn on your workouts (this always seems to surprise some people), because though you may feel lighter than air while you're in the moment, you're still kicking those muscle fibers into top form. Follow the fueling advice in Chapter 11 to keep the aches to a minimum. If time permits, treat yourself to a nice massage. You have most definitely earned it.

As before, most I Do moves start in the power position. Stand tall and keep your knees soft. Activate your abs by pulling your navel to your spine and maintain a straight back and tight, firm belly throughout the moves. If your form starts to fall apart, stop. Do fewer reps with perfect form and gradually build up to the suggested number. That's especially important with the athletic I Do moves because poor form increases your risk for injury. In keeping with the Show It Love philosophy, the I Do Woman Warrior series begins with a trio of core exercises that are designed to create energy in the body—warming your core; increasing blood flow; and lubricating your spine, hips, and other joints—so you can perform in a full, powerful range of motion.

The Details

Reps. Perform 12 reps of each move. For single leg moves, perform 12 reps per side for a total of 24. At this point, you should be considerably stronger than when you started with the I Am exercises, so you'll likely find that you can use heavier weights. But don't overdo it. I want you to be able to move fluidly and to really air it out in moves that require jumping and sweeping, so the weight shouldn't be so heavy that it literally weighs you down.

Sets. Aim to perform three sets of each move. If you can only do two, try lowering the weight. If you still find your form falling apart after two sets, that's fine. Stick to two sets until you feel strong enough to add a third. It may take a little more time for your body to adjust to the new demands of I Do. That's perfectly fine and appropriate. Don't rush it.

The weight. Again, the weight you choose should be heavy enough so the final three reps feel very challenging. As you get stronger, the moves will feel easier. When those last reps become a breeze, it's time to increase the load.

Progression. For the first week, perform the routine in traditional strength training fashion, completing all three sets of each exercise before moving on to the next one. Starting with week two, perform the moves as a circuit, completing one set of each move, then immediately going on to the next exercise, completing the entire sequence a total of three times. Every time you increase your weights, go back to traditional three-sets-in-a-row lifting for one week before again performing the routine as a circuit.

Times per week. You will be performing the Woman Warrior exercises three days a week, along with I Do cardio exercises three days a week. See the I Do Workout Log on page 242 for your complete I Do exercise program.

Movement prep. Before starting, do five minutes of light cardio exercise, like jumping rope, light calisthenics, or running in place, to warm up your muscles and get them ready for action.

Lie on your back, lift your legs off the floor at about 45 degrees, and point your toes. Hold a ball in your hands over your chest (any kind will do; if you have no ball, you can even hold a water bottle). Pull your navel to your spine and lift your shoulders off the floor.

THE MOVE: Gimme the Ball

YOU'LL FEEL IT: Throughout the entire rectus abdominis (long abdominal muscle that runs from your ribs to your hips), including the very hard-to-target lower region, and into the obliques. You'll also get a little bonus burn through your thighs.

THE BODY-LOVE BENEFIT: This move will bring out your inner athlete and remind you that being physical is also supposed to be fun.

In one smooth motion, drop your right leg and lift your left leg just enough to pass the ball from one hand to the other between them.

Immediately switch leg positions, passing the ball back through the other way.

Repeat for a full set in each direction.

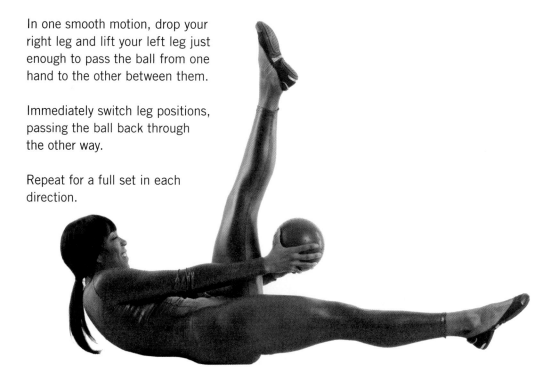

KACY'S COACHING TIPS: Keep your movements controlled. Your legs shouldn't be flailing all over the place. They should move in quick, controlled flicks up and down, just enough to keep the ball bobbing and weaving. Keep your jaw, neck, and shoulders relaxed. All the tension should stay in your core.

Lie on your left side propped up on your left forearm. Cross your ankles by placing your right foot in front of the left, and lift your body off the floor so it forms a straight diagonal line. Place your right hand behind your head so your elbow points toward the ceiling.

THE MOVE: Core Radiance

YOU'LL FEEL IT: In your obliques, abs, back, chest, and shoulders.

THE BODY-LOVE BENEFIT: Sometimes the hardest moves are the smallest. This one forces you to hold your body still against the forces of gravity while performing small, fluid curls. The result is rock-solid stability. You'll be an unbudgeable force in the face of adversity.

Holding this side plank position, contract
your abs and obliques, and curl your right
elbow down across your chest toward
the floor as far as comfortably possible
without dropping out of the plank position.

Return to the starting position. Complete a
set, and then switch sides.

KACY'S COACHING TIPS: You need to keep your core tight and strong to maintain
this pose, but the rest of you should be loose. Relax your face and neck. Keep your
shoulders down away from your ears. Don't allow your hips to sag toward the floor.
Your body should stay completely straight from head to toe.

Stand in the power position with your feet wider than shoulder-width apart. Hold your dowel overhead with your hands also positioned wider than shoulder-width apart, palms facing forward.

THE MOVE: Goddess

YOU'LL FEEL IT: From your toes to your fingertips. This exercise makes every muscle buzz as it challenges stability, strength, and flexibility, all in one sweeping move.

THE BODY-LOVE BENEFIT: This epitomizes the coming together of I Am, I Can, and I Do. It's emotional. It's spiritual. It's *really* physical. Once you have mastered this move, you have arrived!

Bend to the right side, reaching toward the floor with the end of your dowel.

continued »

KACY'S COACHING TIPS: This move is grounded in the energy-channeling philosophies of tai chi, but I've turbocharged it to be performed with a fast rhythm and pace. Once you get it down, it should be one quick, continuous, flowing move.

Now flip the dowel so that the end that was pointing toward the floor is now pointing toward the ceiling.

THE MOVE: Goddess, *continued*

From that position, sweep the dowel to the left across the front of your body until you're bent to the left side, facing forward.

Raise your body back to the starting position. Repeat for a full set starting to the right, and then switch sides.

Stand in the power position with your feet close together. Grasp your dowel with both hands and hold it at chest level, palms facing out.

In one smooth motion, press the dowel straight overhead and lift your right knee straight out in front of you.

THE MOVE: Warrior III

YOU'LL FEEL IT: Where won't you feel it? This crescendo of the Warrior moves strengthens and stretches you from head to toe, channeling toning energy through your shoulders, chest, core, hips, glutes, and thighs.

THE BODY-LOVE BENEFIT: There's a real satisfaction that comes from no longer needing the balancing support of the staff. By raising it off the floor and wielding it like the bad ass you are, it's like screaming, "Yes! I have arrived!"

Pull the dowel back down to chest level while leaning forward slightly and swinging your bent right leg behind you.

Finally, push the dowel straight out, extend your right leg straight back, and dip slightly into your left leg.

Pull the dowel back in, return to a standing position but without lowering your right foot, and immediately press into the next repetition. Complete a full set with your right leg, and then switch sides.

KACY'S COACHING TIPS: Keep your focus. Imagine all the earth's gravitational forces cementing your supporting foot to the floor. Keep yourself completely centered, and let the energy flow through you. It'll keep you from bobbling and losing your balance.

From the power position, lean forward from your hips and grasp the back of a sturdy chair so your back is flat and parallel to the floor.

Raise and extend your right leg straight out behind you, allowing your left leg to bend slightly. Pulse your right leg up and down for a full set.

THE MOVE: Master Blaster

YOU'LL FEEL IT: Boosting your booty. This move hits the glute muscles from every single angle to tighten, tone, and lift that butt like you never thought possible.

THE BODY-LOVE BENEFIT: When your ass is having a good day, you're having a good day! Seriously, so much of our strength as women comes from our "seat" of power located in our lower half. When you build stamina in your hips and glutes, you'll feel like there's no challenge you can't conquer.

Immediately pull your right knee to your chest, and then extend the leg back out for a full set.

Finally, bend your right leg so your knees are in line and your right shin is parallel to the floor.

continued »

KACY'S COACHING TIPS: Keep your glutes contracted and active throughout the entire move. You should not feel this in your lower back. If you do, your glutes are giving out and your form is failing. In that case, start with 8 to 10 reps, and work your way up.

Lift your bent right leg out to the side, extending it straight out at the top of the lift.

Lower and repeat for a full set, and then switch legs.

THE MOVE: Master Blaster, *continued*

Holding a medicine ball with both hands, stand on your right foot and extend your arms directly overhead. Your left thigh should be nearly parallel to the floor.

THE MOVE: Lift It, Love It

continued »

YOU'LL FEEL IT: This move targets those hard-to-hit muscles in your inner and outer thighs as well as your glutes. As a bonus, it fires up your abs and obliques.

THE BODY-LOVE BENEFIT: This balance move not only gets your heart pumping and sculpts your inner and outer thighs, but it also improves your posture and poise, which helps you look confident on the outside even if you don't always feel that way on the inside!

Take a giant step and lunge to the left, dropping the ball to the front of the left foot.

Press back to the starting position.

THE MOVE: Lift It, Love It, *continued*

KACY'S COACHING TIPS: Perform this move as one flowing motion, reaching and lengthening your body in every step of the move. Have fun with it; smile like you're plucking the moon out of the sky and whirling it around your body.

Immediately swing your left leg behind you and to the right, bending both knees into a curtsy while sweeping the ball across the front of your body towards the back foot.

Stand in the power position, legs wide apart, feet pointing out. Clasp your hands in front of your chest with your arms straight out. Quickly bend your knees into a plié-style squat.

THE MOVE: Heel-Click Plié

YOU'LL FEEL IT: In your inner and outer thighs, booty, calves, and core.

THE BODY-LOVE BENEFIT: Nothing, and I mean nothing, activates your fast-twitch muscle fibers—the ones that sculpt all those killer curves—the way ballistic moves like this do. By keeping those fibers ready and active, you'll also find yourself "springing into action" more often in your daily life. Whether you're dashing up and

Without hesitation, spring up into the air, extending your legs and pulling them together to click your heels before opening them wide again as you return to the starting position. Be sure to land with soft knees. As soon as you touch down, dip immediately into your next repetition.

down the stairs at work or dashing for the end zone while you play touch football with your kids, you'll feel fully alive.

KACY'S COACHING TIPS: Think of your legs as big springs. The instant you touch the ground, they should fold and get ready for the next bounce. This movement is intended to be straight up and down, not a forward jump, so aim to take off and land in the same spot.

Stand in the power position with your feet close together, knees soft. Grasp a dumbbell by one end with both hands, and extend your arms directly over your head.

THE MOVE: Tri-Fecta

YOU'LL FEEL IT: In your triceps. The backs of your upper arms will be sending up smoke signals by the final rep.

THE BODY-LOVE BENEFIT: The triceps are our "pushing muscles," which are notoriously flabby on women, because although we do a whole lot of pulling and picking up (which uses the biceps), we don't do much pushing. When I see a

Keeping your upper arms as close to your ears as possible, bend your elbows and drop the weight behind your head.

Keeping your elbows close to your head, fully extend your arms and lift the weight back up.

Complete a full set, and then repeat the move, this time lowering the weight only to the halfway point, so your arms are bent 90 degrees. Complete another full set.

continued »

woman with well-defined triceps, I think, "There's a woman with the power to push back." And in this world, that's a very good thing.

KACY'S COACHING TIPS: Keep those upper arms pinned close to your ears. If you let them flail out to the sides, you lose the effectiveness of the exercise and start stressing your joints. Because you're actually doing 36 reps of this move, err on the lighter side when you pick your weight.

Finally, starting with the weight all the way down behind your head, lift up just to the halfway point, and repeat for another full set.

THE MOVE: Tri-Fecta, *continued*

226

Stand in the power position with your feet close together, knees soft. Hold a dumbbell in each hand, palms facing out.

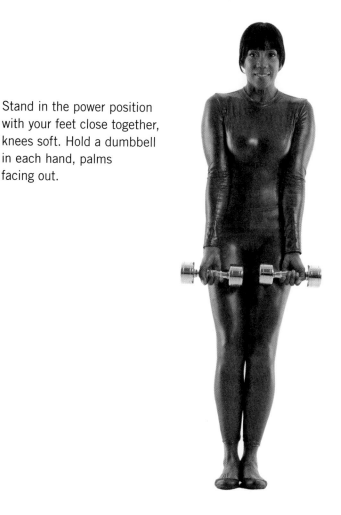

THE MOVE: Double Bi

continued »

YOU'LL FEEL IT: Through your entire biceps and into your shoulders.

THE BODY-LOVE BENEFIT: This move etches a pretty line between your biceps and your shoulders. But more important, it builds endurance in your arms so you can cradle small children and hold on tight to the ones you love.

Keeping your elbows close to your sides, bend your arms so your forearms are extended straight out in front of your body at waist height, palms facing up.

Squeeze your biceps and lift the weights up to your shoulders.

THE MOVE: Double Bi, *continued*

KACY'S COACHING TIPS: Pretend your elbows are Krazy Glued to your sides so you completely isolate your biceps. Don't "assist" with the move by hoisting your torso backward as you lift. Keep the rest of your body still as a statue but completely relaxed.

Lower back to the starting position and immediately rotate your arms out to your sides; curl the weights back up to the outsides of your shoulders.

Continue alternating for a full set.

Stand in the power position, feet close together, knees slightly bent. Hold dumbbells in your hands with your arms extended down in front of you, palms facing your thighs.

Keeping your arms extended, raise them straight out in front of your body until they are parallel to the floor.

THE MOVE: Open with Power

YOU'LL FEEL IT: In your shoulders, back, and chest.

THE BODY-LOVE BENEFIT: It's fitting that you wrap up your final workout on your Show It Love journey with this move that puts the polish on the beautiful sculpture you've worked so hard to create. Goddess, indeed.

Squeeze your shoulder blades together, open your arms straight out to the sides, and rotate your wrists so your body forms a T, palms facing forward.

Keep arms in the up position, squeeze your chest muscles, and pull the weights together in front of your body. Open back to the T position.

Repeat for a full set.

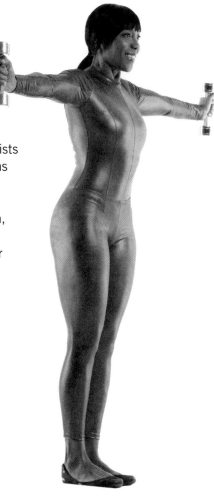

KACY'S COACHING TIPS: Keep your jaw and neck relaxed and your shoulders down during this move. Because it fully and continuously engages your deltoids, it doesn't take much weight to get the job done, so err on the lighter side for weights.

Woman Warrior Inspiration

~ *Oshun* ~

When I need to go out and be slammin', I look to Oshun, the absolute *queen* of feminine beauty and art. The Yoruban goddess of love, she rules the realm of sensual pleasures and revels in jewelry, dress, and self-adornment. Nothing makes her happier than an artfully decorated home, and even a plain old coffee cup thrills her if it's handcrafted with an eye toward fine aesthetics. Her symbols are mirrors, jewelry, honey, feathered fans, and golden silk.

But make no mistake, Oshun is not about petty vanity. She's about the celebration of creativity and beauty in this world. So it pleases her when we honor ourselves enough to care for our appearance and adorn ourselves. Known as Oxum in Brazil, Oshun is also regarded as the ruler of the "sweet" waters, like rivers, brooks, and streams. I can tell you this, her blessings flow freely, making this world a more beautiful, peaceful place. Raise your remarkable body up to her as you tone, tighten, and rejoice in your amazing self!

Remember to stretch. You can repeat the simple yet highly effective stretches on pages 70–78 in the I Am section.

13

Keep On Keeping On

Fuel Your Mind, Muscles, and Motivation for Life

Comfort—it's a great quality for couches, mattresses, and pajamas, but not for workouts. We grow and get results only when we regularly push ourselves outside of our comfort zone. More important, it's that constant tension of challenge that fuels our inner athlete and helps maintain motivation, not just for a few weeks or months but for the rest of our lives.

Case in point: Yoko Ono. I had the honor of training her as she prepared to celebrate her 70th birthday. Here is a woman who has had great loss in her life; who has faced tremendous amounts of derision and adversity; who has had the rug pulled out from beneath her feet so many times, it's a miracle she's still standing. But each time, she gets up, dusts herself off, and moves forward, breaking new, challenging ground. When she wanted help with her training, she could have simply paid for private sessions in the comfort of her living room, but she chose to come to me. I could tell it was uncomfortable for her to walk into the club and work out in the glaring spotlight of a hundred staring eyes. But she made the choice to share herself and risk looking vulnerable and unsure as she learned and attempted challenging physical moves. It is that I Do spirit that not only gives her an amazing, lithe, beautiful body as she enters her eighth decade of life but also keeps her such a vital, relevant artist, most recently performing at the 2006 Olympic ceremonies in Turino, Italy, more than 25 years after John Lennon's death. There's no question that this woman has the means to retreat and retire to a life of leisure on the shores of any ocean she chooses, yet she opts to stay in New York City and keep making waves all her own.

So it's time to tap into your own inner athlete and Yoko Ono (or whoever your strong female role model may be). You've built a solid foundation of emotional, spiritual, and physical strength, so you can safely press forward, taking your body and mind and soul places they've never been!

Just Jump (and Let Your Wings Appear)

That means it's time to go back to your goals and do some updating. If you have not already broken out of your comfort zone, do it now. In the next month, I want you to try one thing that is completely different from the activities you usually gravitate toward. It shouldn't be something you know will come easily either. I have one client who will try only things she knows she can succeed at and look good at while she does them. That's not how you grow as a person. It's also not how your physical appearance and abilities improve. You have to spend some time working on what's hard. If you're not flexible, go ahead and take an introductory yoga class. Uncoordinated? Try a dance class. I just did this recently myself. I signed up for tango lessons. Although I have a strong dance background, this is completely different from how I'm used to moving, and I am really struggling. It's uncomfortable for me to have to work so hard publicly at something that it seems like I should be good at. But that's the point. It's the discomfort and the work that's going to make me grow and ultimately build not just my body but also my confidence and character.

If you feel afraid, remember that the Show It Love system is always there as your safety net. Let this book be a constant tool for you as you move along your path. If, as you wade into uncomfortable waters, you start feeling less sure of yourself, take a trip back through I Am to regain your emotional bearings. The exercises (physical and otherwise) in this book are not once and done. They're relevant and useful each time you forge ahead into brave new territory as a woman. Each time you circle back through your I Am, I Can, I Do journey, you'll only get stronger in mind, body, and spirit.

So don't be the girl in the gym who wants only to look good and feel like a pro at everything she does. Every time you feel yourself settling into a comfortable routine, break out of that mold and keep growing. Here are just a few things clients have been inspired to try (and often ended up loving):

- Gymnastics (Yep, you read that right. A 40-something-year-old woman jumps and tumbles, and she loves it!)
- Flamenco dancing
- Martial arts
- Running club
- Triathlon (There's that word again; a great challenge for damn near everyone to try.)
- African dance
- Tennis
- Indoor soccer (There are dozens of leagues looking for women.)
- Ice-skating (Even speed skating! It gives you an amazing workout.)
- Kayaking
- Golf
- Backpacking

The secret to having a positive experience (the main measure of success) is trying the activity at the appropriate level. That is, don't set yourself up for abject failure by stepping into an advanced tennis clinic if you don't know what 40–love means (you'll soon find out). Find an environment that is beginner-friendly. Then walk in with an open mind and your ego firmly tucked away in your back pocket. Be prepared to struggle and maybe even look a little silly. From that starting point, every success you have will leave you feeling like the winner you are for having the courage to try.

Track Your Accomplishments

One of the fringe benefits of taking on a fresh new challenge is that you have nowhere to go but up. You can make great strides in just a few weeks. If you don't already keep an exercise journal to chart your progress, I highly recommend that you do, so you can clearly see each time you reach a personal best—whether it's running three miles in 30 minutes, reaching the floor in a challenging yoga pose, or making it through three full sets of all your Woman Warrior exercises for the first time.

The journal doesn't have to be anything elaborate or fancy—just a calendar-style book where you can record what you've done each day and how you felt. Ideally, the journal shouldn't dictate every last detail you should put in; it should leave space for you to write down what's important to you—the weather, your mood, how you looked and felt in your new gym pants, it's all relevant. My cowriter, Selene, has kept exercise journals for nearly a decade and finds them an endless source of motivation, perspective, and often pride. "There's nothing like flipping through all those pages and reflecting on the challenges and triumphs," she says. "It's also a concrete reminder that life's not perfect, and even after bad spells when I couldn't exercise, with persistence and patience, I was able to keep making progress over the long haul. Journaling is also very motivating, because nobody wants to open her journal and see a bunch of blank pages! You want to be able to write down that you did *something.*"

As you record your workouts, keep an eye out for places where you'd like to improve your performance and work on those areas. Most important, highlight the accomplishments that make you proud. If you really, really didn't want to go to the gym one day but dragged yourself out the door and ended up having an incredible workout, stick a gold star in your journal. Being able to look back and see your notes from that day will inspire you to move next time your motivation is MIA.

How Much Is Enough?

That's what everyone wants to know: "How much cardio do I have to do?" Honestly, to fully honor your physical self and reap maximum health and body-shaping benefits, you should be doing at least 30 minutes a day. But if you can't, at least try to add a day whenever you can. It's good for your muscles and your mind. And it's most definitely the Show It Love way.

Your ultimate goal should be to aim for an hour of physical activity most days of the week (your Woman Warrior routines count!). Don't panic. It's easier than you think. Just take the advice I gave you in the I Am section and spread your sessions out a little when time is tight. My cowriter, Selene, swears by getting on her Spinning bike for 15 to 20 minutes before breakfast a few times a week. "I don't do anything crazy. Just put on my iPod and sit and spin my legs for four songs. It gets my blood pumping and cranks up my fat-burning enzymes, so I ramp up my calorie-burning metabolism right out of the gate. Then I'll lift or run or do another activity later in the afternoon,

Woman Warrior Inspiration

~ *Hsi Wang Mu* ~

The Show It Love system honors your body as an eternal entity, not just a physical presence in the here and now. That's why I love Hsi Wang Mu, the Taoist goddess of immortality. Like so many of us, Hsi Wang Mu started at ground zero, often finding herself in trouble. But over time, she discovered her strength and rose to great heights as the empress of all divinities. Despite tremendous power, she never lost touch with her feminine self and always embodied the spirit of yin, the feminine aspect of nature and the world. She protected the spirits of all Taoist priestesses, appearing in their dreams, watching over them, and helping them. She embraced the power of women and took particular care of women who were single and women who lived outside the bounds of conventional life. She believed in embracing each woman's unique identity. By accessing the power of Hsi Wang Mu, you will strengthen your own purpose, spirit, and identity and gain a greater ability to further your fitness goals over your whole life.

when I have a break in my schedule. It's a sneaky way to get in a lot of exercise without feeling like you're making a huge time commitment."

On days when you're doing high-intensity cardio, you clearly don't have to crank out an hour of exercise. But you should still make a point of getting out of your chair and moving more throughout the day so you're not just sitting there in one position letting your back and legs get stiff and sore. This can be as simple as walking the dog in the evening after work or going out for a short walk during the day. Even window-shopping counts if you don't stop and stare at all the new shoes too long. At this point in your body-love transformation, you should be automatically thinking "active" as you go through your day, always looking for excuses to stretch your legs and move your body. After all, you can't reach the body of your dreams planted on your ass.

Not the End

Congratulations on completing your journey through Show It Love. By now you realize that, though you're leaner, stronger, and more confident, you never really reach the end of the road. There's more to discover around every bend. Sometimes there are detours, often roadblocks. And when there are, that's when you can turn back to this book and use it as your map to find your way over, around, or straight through the obstacles that life places in your way.

In Your Daily Get-Through-Anything Guide at the end of the book, you'll find shortcuts to provide a quick I Am, I Can, I Do boost when you need it most. You can also go back and revisit the Milestone quizzes to be sure your emotional and spiritual self is still on a positive path. My hope is that you can use this book as a tool to keep you strong, healthy, and empowered as you live and grow through your life.

Now go take on the world!

I Do Milestones

Are You Really Doing It?

Here you are poised at the finish line. Just a few more steps and you'll have completed the entire Show It Love system! At this point, it's crucial to do a little self-examination. Are you squarely on the path to lifelong fitness? Have you lived to your fullest through your body? Or have you let your body hate hold you back? Have you truly (and finally) found peace and happiness inside your skin? Before you close this book, you need to know instinctively how to keep making goals, accomplish those goals, and continue to push and grow and keep the results coming. You're ready to move into maintenance mode only when you wake up feeling competent, confident, and strong, when you're no longer afraid of looking foolish but actively seek opportunities to try—and maybe even fail at—new physical challenges. You should be comfortable eating like an athlete and giving your body what it needs when it needs it.

Here are some important questions to see if you've reached the milestones for the I Do portion of the Show It Love program. You should consider your journey complete when you can answer the following questions positively and honestly. (No matter how you score on this quiz, remember that the most important thing you can do is to keep using this book to remind you, as needed, of some truly powerful ways to ground yourself mentally so that you can really do all you want physically.)

1 **What is your fitness routine?**
   a. The same set of exercises almost every day.
   b. A varying set of exercises but at the same level of difficulty.
   c. A routine that changes depending on my inner needs and the parts of my body I want to work on.

When you look at your body in the mirror, what do you see?

a. I still see faults that are unsatisfying to me.

b. I see gradual, pleasing improvement.

c. I feel that I still have more potential, that I can become stronger and fitter in my training.

What is your relationship to food (honestly)?

a. I'm still ridden with guilt because I occasionally fly off the program.

b. It's still deeply important to me—something I focus on a bit too much.

c. Food is integrated into my respect for and enjoyment of my body.

A friend suggests taking a salsa dance class. What is your reaction?

a. No freakin' way. I have two left feet and no desire to look like an idiot.

b. I give a nervous nod, but if I can find a legitimate way out, I'm relieved.

c. Hell, yeah. I know it'll be tough, but I can't wait to master some new moves to throw down on the dance floor.

You pull a muscle in your new kickboxing class. What's your reaction?

a. I throw in the towel, thinking, "This exercise stuff's not for me."

b. I look forward to getting back to class sometime but use it as an excuse to hit the couch with a stack of "Sex and the City" DVDs.

c. I make a note of what caused the injury (so I don't repeat it), then keep moving the rest of my body while giving the muscle time to mend.

When you see an exceptionally beautiful movie actress, what do you do?

a. Compare myself to her and feel as if I'll never get there.

b. See her physical attractiveness as a goal I can achieve with time.

c. Forget to compare myself to her at all and simply enjoy her (and my own body) for what she is.

If your answers are mostly a, *you need to revisit the I Am section. If they're mostly* b, *repeat some of the routines set out in I Can. If they're mostly* c, *congratulate yourself and your marvelous body, and keep at it!*

I Do Workout Log

You have made the commitment and are making it happen! Keep the momentum rolling strong through the final section of your I Am, I Can, I Do journey. At this point, you shouldn't just be recording your workouts but also creating some of your own.

Your first week of I Do should look like this:

MONDAY	TUESDAY	WEDNESDAY	THURSDAY	FRIDAY	SATURDAY	SUNDAY
Woman Warrior, 3 sets Stretches	Cardio, 30–40 minutes or 20 minutes high-intensity intervals*	Woman Warrior, 3 sets Stretches	Cardio, 30–40 minutes or 20 minutes high-intensity intervals*	Woman Warrior, 3 sets Stretches	Cardio, 30–40 minutes or 20 minutes high-intensity intervals*	Off

*Try a new class, blend your own workout, or train for an event.

Use the log sheet on the next page to track your progress.

I Do Log Sheet

THE MOVE	NUMBER OF SETS/ NUMBER OF REPS	I FELT . . .
Gimme the Ball	_____	_____
Core Radiance	_____	_____
Goddess	_____	_____
Warrior III	_____	_____
Master Blaster	_____	_____
Lift It, Love It	_____	_____
Heel-Click Plié	_____	_____
Tri-Fecta	_____	_____
Double Bi	_____	_____
Open with Power	_____	_____

THE CARDIO	NUMBER OF MINUTES	I FELT . . .
New class	_____	_____
My cardio blend	_____	_____
My intervals	_____	_____
Other _____	_____	_____

Your Daily Get-Through-Anything Guide

Life is filled with curveballs—both good and bad. Your boyfriend dumps you by e-mail. You get the job of your dreams . . . and are scared to death. Or you, your hair, and your backside are just not having a good day. The old you might have run to the refrigerator for some solace and support. The new I Am, I Can, I Do you just goes out and runs!

You now know the emotional power of exercise—how every Master Blaster leg raise can lift your spirit as well as your glutes. You can tap into that power to knock every curveball life pitches your way straight out of the park. Let the following routines be your guide for the Woman Warrior moves that will help most in specific situations.

General Guidelines

For every workout:

- Warm up with 10 to 15 minutes of your choice of cardio (such as running or marching in place, walking on the treadmill, or riding an exercise bike).
- Do each move in the order given, and perform 12 reps on each side, where applicable. Complete each circuit three times.
- Rest 15 to 30 seconds between each move and 1 minute between each circuit.
- Depending on your fitness level, do the workouts three to four times a week, as needed.

You Got Dumped

These moves will tap into your inner energy and help you feel your raw beauty and power. Do this circuit, hit the showers, and go out and show the world your beautiful self! You won't need that old flame to know you're smokin' hot.

Fire in the Belly (page 48)

Flip, Squat, Press (page 58)

Duke Curtsy (page 54)

Inner Thigh Toner (page 153)

Push, Pull, Kickback (page 61)

Double Bi (page 227)

Swaying in the Breeze (page 70)

You've Been Fired, Now What?

No matter how we try to convince ourselves that we are more than our work, so much of our self-worth is wrapped up in what we do from nine to five. When your professional world is rocked, this circuit will help you strengthen your emotional self and feel confident as you move forward.

Show Some Love (page 46)

Open with Power (page 230)

Warrior I (page 52)

Side Bow (page 50)

Lift It, Love It (page 219)

Plié Drag (page 56)

Tri-Fecta (page 224)

Fuel to the Fire (page 162)

Power Plank (page 145)

Swaying in the Breeze (page 70)

Your Ass Is Having a Bad Day

When your butt is dragging, it brings the rest of you down with it. This glute-kicking circuit is just what you need to give you and your backside a lift.

Warrior II (page 149)

NY Booty Lift (page 158)

Master Blaster (page 216)

Lift It, Love It (page 219)

Flip, Squat, Press (page 58)

Running Goddess (page 156)

Deep Hip Drop (page 77)

Figure 4 Sit-Back (page 76)

You're Bored and Feeling Unfulfilled

Life is not all champagne and roses for anyone. Even the celebrities I work with sometimes feel bored and unfulfilled (the glamorous life isn't always what it's cracked up to be). During these melancholy spells, you need to dig inside yourself for strength and meaning rather than waiting for life to make a special delivery. Get your mojo working in the right direction with this self-inspiring circuit.

Warrior I (page 52)

Warrior II (page 149)

Warrior III (page 214)

Goddess (page 210)

Lift It, Love It (page 219)

Open with Purpose (page 66)

Fuel to the Fire (page 162)

Tri-Fecta (page 224)

Fire in the Belly (page 48)

Gimme the Ball (page 206)

Swaying in the Breeze (page 70)

You're Ready to Make a Change

Any change you want to make, no matter how positive, will be met with some resistance—both internal and external—because change means leaving the comfortable and familiar and breaking new, unknown ground. Prepare yourself to push ahead with this powerful, high-energy circuit.

Warrior I (page 52)

Goddess (page 210)

Plié Drag (page 56)

NY Booty Lift (page 158)

Heel-Click Plié (page 222)

Double Bi (page 227)

Push, Pull, Kickback (page 61)

Fuel to the Fire (page 162)

Power Plank (page 145)

Gimme the Ball (page 206)

Seated Twist (page 73)

You're Kicking a Bad Habit

You gotta break a sweat and get some feel-good hormones going when you're trying to quit nicotine or another addictive drug or behavior. This series pushes you right out of the gate to blow off built-up stress, then it winds down to help you find inner calm and stability.

Flip, Squat, Press (page 58)   Warrior I (page 52)

Lift It, Love It (page 219)   Show Some Love (page 46)

Heel-Click Plié (page 222)

Your Kids Are Sick, and You Haven't Worked Out in a Week

When you're out of your routine and out of sorts, you need a head-to-toe tune-up to put you on the path again. This simple circuit will get you back on the right track in a snap.

Show Some Love (page 46)   Bend and Extend (page 74)

Warrior II (page 149)   Gimme the Ball (page 206)

Duke Curtsy (page 54)   Seated Twist (page 73)

Inner Thigh Toner (page 153)

You're Alone and Feeling Lonely

Get out of the house and go where the action is. Build some positive momentum with this circuit, then hit the gym for cardio or a sculpting class. Or take a gym tour if you're not a member.

Show Some Love (page 46)   Warrior III (page 214)

Warrior I (page 52)   Heel-Click Plié (page 222)

Warrior II (page 149)

Your Class Reunion Is in Eight Weeks

Get ready to strike while your motivation is hot! This all-out I Am, I Can, I Do assault will prepare you emotionally, spiritually, and (what you're really looking for, I know) physically to face your past with true presence.

Creative Curl (page 142)

NY Booty Lift (page 158)

Gimme the Ball (page 206)

Figure 4 Sit-Back (page 76)

Fire in the Belly (page 48)

Fuel to the Fire (page 162)

Core Radiance (page 208)

Tri-Fecta (page 224)

Power Plank (page 145)

Serve It Up (page 64)

Power Press (page 160)

Open with Power (page 230)

Inner Thigh Toner (page 153)

Open with Purpose (page 66)

Lift It, Love It (page 219)

Staff Side Bend (page 147)

Master Blaster (page 216)

Show Some Love (page 46)

Warrior I (page 52)

Deep Hip Drop (page 77)

Warrior II (page 149)

Swaying in the Breeze (page 70)

Warrior III (page 214)

You've Got the Baby-Weight Blues

You're thrilled with the new life you've created but less than excited about not having your old body back yet. Every woman who's had a baby has been there. This circuit tones and strengthens all those "baby-weight" spots in your hips, thighs, and core and reminds you to celebrate the amazing power of the body you're in.

Warrior I (page 52)

Show Some Love (page 46)

Duke Curtsy (page 54)

Side Bow (page 50)

Lift It, Love It (page 219)

Fire in the Belly (page 48)

Flip, Squat, Press (page 58)

Creative Curl (page 142)

Double Bi (page 227)

Swaying in the Breeze (page 70)

Push, Pull, Kickback (page 61)

You Need to Be Red-Carpet Ready for Your Special Event

You want to look and feel like the world is at your feet when the cameras start clicking. This high-intensity circuit will force you to dig deep and push yourself emotionally, spiritually, and physically to emerge with the body of your dreams.

Warrior I (page 52)

Warrior II (page 149)

Warrior III (page 214)

Inner Thigh Toner (page 153)

Lift It, Love It (page 219)

NY Booty Lift (page 158)

Bend and Extend (page 74)

Running Goddess (page 156)

Figure 4 Sit-Back (page 76)

Tri-Fecta (page 224)

Double Bi (page 227)

Push, Pull, Kickback (page 61)

Open with Purpose (page 66)

Open with Strength (page 164)

Goddess (page 210)

Fire in the Belly (page 48)

Creative Curl (page 142)

Core Radiance (page 208)

Power Plank (page 145)

Power Press (page 160)

Swaying in the Breeze (page 70)

Show Some Love (page 46)

You Overindulged

Sometimes that little Friday indulgence ends up stretching into Sunday night. Undo the damage with this energetic circuit that reminds you of the athlete inside and raises your heart rate for a calorie-burning boost.

Heel-Click Plié (page 222)

Lift It, Love It (page 219)

Bend and Extend (page 74)

Master Blaster (page 216)

NY Booty Lift (page 158)

Warrior I (page 52)

Power Press (page 160)

Fire in the Belly (page 48)

Creative Curl (page 142)

Gimme the Ball (page 206)

Seated Twist (page 73)

Index